SURVIVING WITHOUT ROMANCE

SURVIVING WITHOUT ROMANCE

AFRICAN WOMEN TELL THEIR STORIES

MARY LOU CUMMINGS

HERALD PRESS
Scottdale, Pennsylvania
Waterloo, Ontario

Library of Congress Cataloging-in-Publication Data
Cummings, Mary Lou.
Surviving without romance : African women tell their stories / Mary Lou Cummings.
p. cm.
ISBN 0-8361-3538-5
1. Women—Africa, Sub-Saharan—Case studies. 2. Women—Africa, Sub-Saharan—Religious life—Case studies. I. Title.
HQ1787.C85 1991
305.42'0967—dc20 90-48573
CIP

The paper used in this publication is recycled and meets the minimum requirements of American National Standard for Information Sciences—Permanence of Paper for Printed Library Materials, ANSI Z39.48-1984.

Library of Congress Catalog Number: 90-48573
International Standard Book Number: 0-8361-3538-5
Printed in the United States of America
Cover and book design by Gwen Stamm/Cover art by Ugandan batik artist, K. Njagala

1 2 3 4 5 6 7 8 9 10 96 95 94 93 92 91 90

To Bob, Chris, and Lisen, partners in the project.
Without their help, ideas, and encouragement, this project would never have been possible.

To all the African women who showed me how to live above *circumstances, and to do it with style, humor, and song.*

Contents

Author's Preface

Dr. Joyce Brothers has said

> Sigmund Freud asked, "What does a woman want?!" He need not ask today. We all know the answer. . . . A woman wants everything a man wants. Success and power and status and money. Love and marriage and children. Happiness. Fulfillment.

African and American women want the same things. But we live in cultures that define us, that enclose most of us in boundaries of the possible. And so, as one might expect, African and American women look for what they want in different ways and in different places.

In North America, romantic love is touted as the peg on which to hang life. Lois Wyse said, "There is nothing that matters except the two of you and the value of the time you spend together and what you can give each other in terms of emotional support." Love affairs or "meaningful relationships," while no longer assumed to be lifelong, are still a prime American motivator if one can believe our advertising psychologists.

African women make no apologies for their sense that the prime love relationship in life is that between mother and child. A husband is certainly an emotional support system. But he is rarely the soul's twin, the cherisher of my deepest self, that Americans idealistically describe him to be. He is an authority figure, a provider, and gives the family identity in his clan. African women respect their husbands, but they love their children.

African women would be puzzled indeed to hear Lois Wyse's description of what life is about. Life is about food, water, fuel, and making sure the babies stay healthy. Earning school fees for the children so they will get an education and be successful. Weather and crops. Relationships with the others in the village. Walking to work together. Singing, laughing, cracking jokes. Friendship, sharing when a relative has a need. Praying, talking to God as though in the same room, trusting that the next life will abolish pain and sorrow.

An African woman's life is filled with love. She will move heaven and earth to do what she can for her husband, children, relatives, and village. Her life is rich with relationships. But romance is hardly an expectation. There are few compliments, gifts, or candlelight dinners. Husbands do not say, "I love you."

She does not expect to talk about her own needs to her husband. That is the role of a friend. She does not expect to be "in love" with the man chosen for her to marry, although she may have known him or considered him a good prospect. In some cases, she did not even see him before marriage.

Peasant cultures the world over do not count on something as flimsy as infatuation to cement a lifetime contract between two unlike people. They count on relationships between two congenial families. If one or both marriage partners is unstable, there will still be a dependable family support system, a strong clan. The clan will continue to build itself, to grow strong.

The woman actually marries a clan more than a husband. That is why a new widow, if still young enough to bear children, is offered a levirate marriage by the clan. This means she will receive a relative to take her husband's place, so she can continue to have children.

It is hard for us to understand women who survive, and do so quite happily, without romance. We tend to feel pity or superiority. Our culture tells us, quite insistently, that to be whole a woman needs a lover—and one who will truly understand her, at that.

Other cultures, I believe, substitute other things through which women can feel happy and fulfilled. An obvious one is work. African women take pride in their work, although it is arduous and never ending. Farmers particularly see an immediate return on their labor. Their families depend on them to eat and to survive.

African women find joy in relationships with their own children, their fellow Christians, and the villagers among whom they live. They are seldom alone, whether carrying water or washing clothes, and two or three African women can transform the simplest task into a party.

Their relationship with God is often simple, immediate, and direct. And their belief in the next world permeates their endurance of this one.

When several women said to me at various times, "Jesus is my husband," I almost felt it was blasphemous. Then I read Isaiah 54:5, which says, "Your Maker is your husband." I began to believe, after many interviews, that African women had found one key to happiness. Their expectations of other people were not idealistic. They knew better than to pin their hopes for happiness on one other person.

Instead, they pinned their hopes on God and God's promises. It was in that relationship that they grew to be free. Jesus was their husband in that he loved them unconditionally and rose from the dead, promising them eternal life as well. Jesus gave them a place, a name, an identity, and a calling.

As you meet women in this book, it is my hope that you will see in them the strength and optimism and joy of life I saw. You will not see, as I did, the proud posture, the athletic gait of a woman sure of her body and her own muscular strength. But perhaps you will see past the differences in culture, past the history that separates us, to the open hearts that they offer us in telling us their stories.

—Mary Lou Cummings
Quakertown, Penna.

CHAPTER

Nairobi, Kenya

1. At the Airport

"Lean into it," my friend Marian advised, as she hugged me good-bye at JFK airport. "Lean into it!"

I pictured myself leaning into a gale, the wind pushing against me, my shoulders hunched against the wet and the dark. I pictured my shoulders gradually straightening and my head lifting with the exhilaration of being out on a stormy night while ordinary people sat at home, warm and listless in front of TV sets. My adventure was just beginning, and the fear and excitement enlivened all my senses.

But I pushed aside the images my overactive brain threw at me. I had to pay attention. There was no storm—only a plane to catch. Outside, the dreary New York twilight dimmed in drizzling rain. Lights flashed on.

"Stay close," I told the children, although they were so weighed down they couldn't go far. Lisen, age six, managed to skip over cracks despite her heavy backpack containing Cabbage Patch doll, art supplies, books and toys. Chris, age twelve, juggled his guitar and a carryon. He was distracted as he ogled teenagers in the crowd and evaluated their sneakers and bizarre outfits. Bob, a large-boned man with gentle quiet manner belying his stormy emotions, was a port in the storm. He can find his way anywhere, like a cat, so I relinquished directions to him. That night, after months of preparations, storing cars, renting the house, saying good-bye to family and friends, he was exhausted but trustworthy.

I felt I must shepherd the luggage—eight suitcases, four carryons, cameras, and tape recorders, all stacked precariously on a groaning cart. Two suitcases apiece didn't seem like much to pack for a whole year. Their load included shoes, jackets, books for home schooling, clothes for growing children, mosquito nets, a miniature pharmacy, and sheets and towels. Now the luggage seemed a mountain of responsibility, all mine. We couldn't afford to lose anything. Money would be tight this year. I clutched my purse, traveler's checks, passports, medical booklets, and addresses.

Airports quickly wrench travelers apart from those who come to send them off. Now our focus was only on finding the gate, intact with children and belongings. Fond farewells of fifteen minutes ago receded completely from my consciousness as I focused on the next procedure. I had to insist my film couldn't go through the X-rays and then endured an electronic frisking for my troublemaking.

We slumped dispirited in a large crowd waiting for the late plane to Amsterdam. Even the children were silent as we all thought own worried thoughts, facing the now black airport windows which reflected our images back at us. Tall, balding husband, short, blonde wife, two blonde children—one tiny-boned girl and an athletic, active son. An ordinary family—they should turn around and go back home while they can instead of stepping into the unknown for a year.

Chris jabbed me. His eyes were sharp; he saw everything. "Look, Mom, at that man's luggage. Just like ours."

Two young men sat nearby, each with a travel bag with a Mennonite Central Committee (MCC) logo like ours. A spark lighted our sagging spirits. We all perked up to ask them questions. Yes, they too were going to Nairobi. The same organization was sending us. We laughed at the coincidences. Such serendipity brought a much-needed flash of awareness that the Holy Spirit was here in the airport with us.

Don Martin, a doctor, headed to the small, church hospital and town in Tanzania that we had often read about. Conrad Martin was an accountant who would live in Shirati, too. I looked at them—young, unmarried, full of the adventure before them, reading guidebooks for their stopover in Europe. I felt a twinge of envy. That is how I had envisioned myself—fresh out of college, full of idealism, teaching in Africa.

Instead Bob and I married and circumstances led us into suburban teaching jobs, ministries in the church, a house, and, later, children. Now here I was, a middle-aged mother, loaded down with schoolbooks and Pepto-Bismol, dragging my family after me to pursue my dream twenty years later.

They plied us with questions, curious. "Bob has a sabbatical," we told them, "and Mary has been waiting years for an opportunity to finally experience Africa. This is her chance."

"I'm planning to visit and interview women who are leaders in the local churches in East Africa," I told the men. "So often the women have been overlooked. If I find a team of interested people, we can collect stories, affirm local leaders, and hold up women as role models to the young. It would be a gift to the women to have a set of tape cassettes full of stories about themselves and the way they overcame their individual struggles through Christ."

"And MCC is backing you?" they asked. They knew this arm of the Mennonite and Brethren in Christ churches is deeply involved in international development. But the activity is usually more institutional, involving schools, hospitals and training programs.

"Yes," I said. "They believe that the women of Africa can be a real source of support to each other. But they need a chance to interact beyond their own tribes, to experience a sense of sisterhood across Africa. These stories might be a first step in that direction. So few projects really benefit women in the churches. And yet women are often the ones who make things happen in the church.

"I know I'll experience some real glitches. Everyone tells me things don't always proceed smoothly or as one expects in Africa," I laughed at their doubtful expressions.

"But I want the interviews to be an affirmation of the women chosen by their groups. Even if nothing else comes of it. For once in their lives, these Christian women who have been the strength of the churches should be acknowledged, blessed. If the interview can do that, then I'll have succeeded. Of course, I also want to get the tapes made in local languages, so that they have something to show for it, to use together. But I'll have to learn how to do that."

I always felt nervous when I explained my tentative procedures to people. But I was at least sure of my goals. I had edited a book of biographies of North American churchwomen back in 1978. Back then, none of us were sure our churches had women worth writing about. But since then much more had been written and collected. And women's attitudes about themselves had changed dramatically. There were, of course, stories everywhere once we looked.

Conrad and Don would go to Swahili school, then travel to a small Tanzanian mission station to live. We would visit them there in six months. We swapped a few Swahili words and anecdotes we had heard about the work there.

All of us got animated. We laughed and anticipated together. We exchanged bits of information. There was electricity in the air once more, a sense of adventure. God was present in that airport in the form of kindred spirits, former strangers open to sharing their dreams, their ideals. Such moments happened again and again throughout our year in Africa. They are among my overriding impressions. No matter where one goes, fellow Christians immediately recognize something in each other, and one feels at home.

The six of us boarded the plane together, laughing and talking like old friends. Finally Bob and I sank with relief into our seats and buckled up. Across the aisle Chris and Lisen were wide awake, heads snapping in all directions. Now there was no more to be done. We could sit back.

I fiddled with my earphone dials. Soon the majestic strains of Rachmaninoff's concerto came crashing about my head. *Just like a 1950s B-movie,* I thought, *the grand finale as the plane lifts*. Giggles rose in me like bubbles of champagne as the plane took off to the tune of clashing symbols and grand violins. "Not the finale," I corrected the invisible director, laughing, "Just the beginning!"

2. Life in Nairobi

The house which would be our home for three months was one story, made of gray stone, and the rectangular metal windows were crossed with metal traceries to keep out thieves. On either side were large apartment houses, shaded by high walls and trees. The only evidence of their mixed white, Indian, and black populations was a continual undercurrent of sound—chickens squawking, babies crying, engines revving, and Swahili greetings.

Inside our house, however, it was quiet. The walls were crammed with African art work, mementos, and shelves of English, French, and German books. There were polished wood parquet floors and a sense of European graciousness. The table was laid with ironed linens.

"Come see," Lisen whooped. She had already found a tiny yard behind our veranda, which was protected by a metal grill. It bloomed thickly with red calla lilies, purple bougainvillaea, and pink roses. Tiny, fluorescent purple birds sipped pollen from the poinsettias, and yellow weaver birds swooped and fussed about their inverted straw nests.

Chris found a cat who seemed to feel a territorial ownership of his bedroom. He was delighted.

Grubby and exhausted as we all were, we wanted to chuckle and hug each other.

Our commitment to house-sit this home for a Swiss family on leave in Europe meant we had to pay the servants' salaries and the utilities. So we were not alone in the house. There was John, a Kenyan of quiet dignity and reserve. He cooked, cleaned, and laundered. It was to him, in our eyes, that the house really belonged. He greeted us in his quiet way, and we all immediately liked him.

Nevertheless, we did not jump around, act silly, and hug each other, as we all wanted to. John was a stranger and he was watching us. In Africa, we found out, one is never alone.

It was 4:00 a.m. "Are you awake?" Bob whispered. I admitted it. "I hear a funny noise!"

I shut my eyes again. Bob was the one who heard noises in the night, children wheezing, dogs howling. He was the one who locked doors, checked windows. He was also the one who eyed all the heavy metal gates and *Mbwa Kali* (Beware of Dog) signs as we drove through this British-Indian suburb of Westlands, Nairobi. He read crime statistics and knew that expatriots and wealthy Indians were targets to be robbed here in Nairobi by gangs wielding *pangas*, or machetes.

It was always my role to say, "Yes, but thieves here aren't violent. They only want our things. They're not crazy like back home."

At this point in our well-rehearsed routine, Bob glanced at my puny five-foot-two-inch frame and took on himself the onerous chore of family protection. I was clearly irresponsible. But tonight both of us stiffened, wide awake. We crawled out of bed and sneaked to the door.

To our relief, a thin beam of light showed under Chris's closed door. Inside we heard the rhythmic slap of cards. He was playing solitaire. "Hi, I'm starved," he greeted us. For two weeks, our bodies remained on Pennsylvania time, and we asked a perplexed John to serve soup for breakfast.

African pantries, well-locked and separate from the kitchen, do not contain snacks, so we made eggs. This was my first chance to take stock of the kitchen without John's presence. It was a Unites States 1940s-style kitchen. It had a gas stove with several broken burners, an old, chipped sink, three saucepans with handles askew, and a cupboard of pretty dishes and bowls for dining room use. It was very clean and neat.

"I think this house is great," Chris said, cheerful now that he had warm food. "I can't believe it's so nice."

"It's an answer to prayer," Bob said fervently. "It'll give us a chance to acclimate slowly and learn the ropes. And you have a whole month to look around before school begins. Students here vacation during August, December and April, and go to school the rest of the year."

"Before Lisen fell asleep tonight, she said, 'Mom, is this REAL-

LY Africa?' I don't think she's convinced." I laughed as I told the story.

But inside I, too, was wondering the same thing.

The August weather, Kenya's winter, was dry, cool and overcast. We welcomed the fireplace after dinner, even though it smoked badly. We shivered in this 5,000 foot altitude. But afternoons were pleasant and all of us wanted to explore. We walked down the paved road, thickly occupied with large, expensive homes and apartment complexes.

The fences hung thick with flowers, and the intense blue sky and heavy, white clouds were beautiful but unfamiliar. Even the smells were strange—heavy, sweet frangipani blossoms, spicy smoke from gardeners burning unfamiliar foliage debris, and whiffs of compost heaps and sewage. Behind fences sit two sets of houses, for masters and servants who live closely twined lives. Conversation, laughter, and children's voices drifted from the smaller houses nearer the road. There was only silence from the larger ones, though the windows were open. There were gates, dogs, and guards —*askaris*—protecting the gates.

We passed Africans who said warmly, "Jambo!" Other faces, of women especially, were closed and pointedly offered no greeting. This was the city, the citadel of old colonial days, the place where Westernism did not heal untold old wounds but varnished over them. Our white skins marked us as "Europeans," as they called us. There was no way to blend in.

During our year there, I never heard anyone say they were from Nairobi. Millions live out their lives there. They earn money and respect, or perhaps just survive, there. But home was always elsewhere, a place to return to someday. As I walked I wondered how much pain and uprootedness and fragmentation was hidden under the "city smarts" and Western dress of the young achievers who populated the city.

I felt some panic as I realized how deep and wide were the gaps between our two cultures. *How will I ever understand,* I thought, *what it is like to come to this city to live without ever having read a book or a map or a road sign?* As it is, Bob and I were having trouble absorbing city know-how. We had just learned that Uhuru Highway and Waiyaki Way were the same street. We made our clumsy tongues practice the new sounds—Machakos, Ngong, Biashara, habari gani, Wambui, Penina—simple towns, streets, hellos, names.

Our house happened to be in walking distance of the homes of other MCC personnel, the MCC office in a shopping center about two kilometers away, and a lovely Mennonite Guest House where interesting Westerners and Africans of all denominations continually came and went.

Bob and I marveled that our prayer for housing was answered in such a way. Not only was it half as expensive as an apartment, but it placed us in a warm Christian community. Without these Westerners to offer comfort when we were victims of a pick-pocket and Philip Okeyo's advice as he accompanied us to notorious immigration offices, our first weeks would have seemed bleak indeed.

Our wealthy Indian neighbors were a closed community, the women not seen much outside their homes. We also felt excluded from the lives of the black servants, who were boisterous and fun-loving with each other but dignified and reserved with whites.

So at first we delighted in new friendships with people like Maynard and Hilda Kurtz, overseers of our project. Quiet and gentle people, they were willing to listen to our dreams and goals and let us work at them in ways comfortable to us. They had been in Africa too long to feel more than guarded optimism for our project. They knew there would be too much work and too little time in the African system, but they never let on.

Instead, Maynard took me to see Kenyan novelist Rebecca Njau, who, in addition to novels, had written some collections of African fables and old stories in which women had been the heroines.

In her bubbly presence, the three of us got excited all over again about the need to collect history before it dies with the elderly ones. We all marveled anew at the amazing resilience and strength of African women.

"That strength was there before colonial times," Rebecca said thoughtfully. "I set out to look at the fables because I wanted to know where that strength had come from!" She cautioned me about drinking water or taking foolish risks when I went out to the villages, for she had gotten deathly ill herself this way.

"Don't give up. If you've come a long, long way and the person you are dying to talk to is gone, just look for someone else, one of the old people. There is always someone to talk to. Keep trying. Don't give up."

I had no idea then just how valuable that advice would be.

Another early friend was Miriam Frey, a single and attractive administrator in the MCC office, who reminded us of Bob's sister. She enthusiastically offered to show Bob how to shop in the markets ("When you buy oil, don't be embarrassed to take the lid off and smell it first, to see if it is rancid"). She showed us how to drive on the left in traffic that made the annual wildebeest migration look orderly. She muttered a lot and radiated anger as she drove, but her reflexes were quick.

Don and Em Yoder, from Ohio, had two teenagers Chris enjoyed. They were lively operators of a neighborhood library and church center in an overcrowded housing area of Nairobi. They delighted us with tons of advice on how to do anything and go anywhere. They would have been undaunted in Antarctica.

Tim Gammell was a tree expert who traveled around Kenya in a battered Suzuki, while Elaine kept their home and three children going at a gallop. A warm and friendly chatterer, she knew how to create love and fellowship wherever she went. She did her aerobics, volunteered at a local hospital, rode the bus with the expatriate children, and created an American neighborhood among the MCC workers.

All these people had children. Chris and Lisen made tenuous connections at first, then real friendships. By the time school began in September, we all felt we belonged.

More free spirited were some of the experts in the outlying areas of Kenya, like Peter and Francis Grill, who came into Nairobi frequently for mail and supplies. They were committed to a new and expensive camel-breeding program.

Camels do not defoliate marginal grasslands as cows do, and fragile land can sustain camel browsers well. So Peter was working with nomadic cattle herders, convincing them to experiment with these new camels instead. He regaled us with tales of camel trains, beautiful Somali maidens, and drinking curdled blood with the Maasai. Chris and I drooled with envy. Bob cringed.

Brian and Ardythe Butler worked in a government school near Isiolo, in the dry north. When they came to Nairobi, they made a beeline for the green Nairobi National Park, a favorite place for birdwatchers.

They often invited us along. One day Chris was along when the Land Rover came upon a giraffe, a beautiful young animal who stood just two feet from their car. While Chris excitedly fumbled with his camera, Brian drove quickly in the opposite direction, pursuing an unusual oxpecker. To this day, Chris sputters in indignation when anyone mentions birdwatching. But Brian had several hundred species on his found list.

There were about fifty co-workers in related Mennonite organizations in and around Nairobi. They met monthly to sing and share together. They were shipmates on a wild and varied sea, each with their own stresses and unique ministries. For those whose job was to offer support services to all the Westerners in East Africa through office work, there was always tension. Should they be devoting themselves to care for whites? Were they insulated in white communities? Finding friends in the African community was unlikely for them without a special niche to fill somewhere.

Bob and Chris made regular shopping forays and practiced with shillings. For Chris bargaining was a game he could put his heart into! His tenacity combined with his natural good humor quickly put him ahead of his tense father in gleaning bargains.

Bob was a generous and sensitive soul who asked workmen, "Are you sure you charged us for that last electric switch?" His impulse was to pay people what they asked and add a tip, sure they were too humble to ask for what they deserved. So the obligatory bargaining was a trial for him. When he had agreed, after haggling, to pay ten shillings for lettuce, then he had to begin all over again for the carrots and the bananas. Chris came home exuberant, full of anecdotes. Bob staggered in exhausted.

The driving lessons were going well but also left their scars on Bob. I was a careful but rather vague driver, often forgetting to think ahead. We both agreed it would be better for me to let Bob and his athletic reflexes handle this chore.

In Nairobi there are no vehicle inspections. Often fast-flowing traffic moves, with only milliseconds to spare, around a broken-down vehicle as though it were harmless flotsam.

In traffic circles, or "roundabouts," as they call them there, three lanes of wild traffic flit in various directions with hair-splitting timing. Cars in the inner left lane, for example, have total right-of-way. This allows them to zigzag across several lanes of traffic. Shattered glass and bits of twisted metal litter these roundabouts.

Having the steering wheel on the right means that one's blind left wheel travels along the often chipped edge of the road, wobbling nervously along a six-inch drop-off where a shoulder has once been. Busses and lorries frequently skitter off these shoulders and flip, resulting in heavy fatalities. Driving in Nairobi is not for the weak-hearted.

While Bob and Chris explored and Lisen played with her new friends, I felt restless. I stalked around the house without any household responsibilities, and I worried.

I spent my time writing letters and planning my upcoming visits to interview church women. I was invited to come to Zaire, Zambia, Zimbabwe, and Tanzania, as well as to Kenyan communities. I found that almost all my major contact people planned to arrive in Nairobi for an annual meeting and we would be able to arrange details then.

So for then there was little to do. I continued my reading and research and learned my way around Nairobi. After months of frantic activity at home, preparing for our departure, I *needed* this time to key down. "Learn to relax," I told myself. "Your role here is as encourager, listener to African women. To do that you will need to be in touch with God's Spirit within. Give yourself two months of relative calm. Pray."

I prayed, but I was not calm. The sensory stimulation around me made my brain pop and crackle. Thoughts exploded like popcorn. Everything was new and I wanted to learn it. I practiced Swahili. I attended a Kenya course at the National Museum and listened to lecturers like Richard Leakey. I had trouble sitting still.

I became increasingly irritable about our house. Though it was beautiful, living in it made its quirks apparent. The water was hot, for example, only at widely unpredictable intervals. One grabbed a shower when one could. The bed sagged badly, and the only way we could sleep was to put the mattress on the floor each night and sneak it back before John noticed. The cat had brought in fleas which bit me savagely on the ankles.

Worst of all was getting used to a servant who worked around me all day, methodically replacing the papers or coffee cups I scattered carelessly. Ceaselessly he cooked and cleaned and laundered. *What does he think of me*, I wondered as I put down my book to take a stack of clean laundry from him, every item ironed into carefully folded rectangles, even underwear. I had never seen our clothes so white.

John took great pride in his work; he was excellent. He served elegant platters of chicken with gravy, deep-fried fish and chips, rhubarb pie with custard and hard-fried eggs, all without any American skittishness about calories or cholesterol. Bob and the children loved the food. They were delighted at the lack of chores and responsibility. If John served something they hated, rather than hurt his feelings they flushed it down the toilet.

John refused to call Bob and me by name. He preferred "Sir" and "Madame." He seemed to feel that this formality also preserved his own dignity. He worked long hours, with great skill, for $60 a month. He lived on the premises, visiting his family in western Kenya twice a year and sending them his savings for school fees. He seemed very loyal to his family back home. He was evidently confident that his wife would raise the family village-style, although he had not lived there for more than fifteen years.

I could not see him work this way without feeling deep guilt about that system. It forces a man to leave his home and family to live on pittance wages simply to make life more comfortable for expatriates. Yet I knew he was glad for this job. There were none to be had out in the country.

To make my guilt worse, John had digestive problems related to a stomach ulcer. He also had a chronic limp and leg pain. If he took consistently the daily medications for which he had prescriptions, they would have cost a third of his month's wages, so he only took them when he was desperate. We were relieved when he asked our advice about getting them from the United States. We are able to supply them for him.

So John's presence was a constant source of ambivalent feelings for me, a reminder of the deep injustices and economic realities around me and my own helplessness.

I worried, too, because it became clear, even after only several weeks, that we could live there for years and never develop any real relationships with Africans. Oh, there were tantalizing glimpses of the real thing. One day, for example, Bob and Chris went to the produce market.

While Bob was paying for some beans, Chris muttered quietly, "Dad, we're the only whites in this whole market! Doesn't that make you a little nervous?"

His dad kept counting out money and said, "Oh, no, to me we're all just people here."

The woman handed them the beans, with an extra wide smile. Unknown to them, she had understood their conversation. They could hear the story being translated in Swahili from stall to stall. In that crowded market, amid the din, a flash of kinship had jumped like lightning from heart to heart. A contact had been made, however fragmentary.

Another day I stood under a hot sun at a nearby bus stop, enroute to downtown Nairobi to run errands. There was a large fair being held on the far side of Nairobi, and after twenty minutes the gathered crowd began to mutter that all the busses must have been diverted to haul the huge crowds there. I struck up a conversation with the middle-aged woman next to me. We agreed to walk the two kilometers to the next bus stop, hoping to find a bus there. Njambi Muturi, or Tabitha, was not pretty. Her face was pitted with smallpox scars, but a fine intelligence flashed in her eyes.

"I used to work for the Mandeleo ya Wanawake (Kenya's large national organization for women)," she told me, "but there was so much internal politics and bickering I got disillusioned. 'We shouldn't be arguing among ourselves,' I would say. 'We should be helping the poorest of the poor.'

"The Wakamba women had to dig in dry creekbeds for water, and we began digging wells for them. I say, 'Give them the priority. No one should be born to suffer at someone else's expense.' We found the women easy to work with. They tend to group together anyway, to get things done.

"For myself, I am the type of woman who can adapt. I could be happy anywhere. That's my attitude.

"I am concerned about homeless children on the streets of Nairobi. We have a children's department under the minister of home affairs, but they are doing nothing. There are not thousands, just hundreds, so it is a manageable number. We could take them in and help them. I often feel like writing to the president and saying, 'Make *me* minister of children!'

"When I worked for the Mandeleo, I used to go up to the tea plantation area. There the women rise as early as 3:00 a.m. to milk. They cook for the children, send them to school, gather food for the livestock, and then go out and pick tea all morning and walk it to the co-op. [It has to be picked and sold before 1:00 p.m.]. Then they walk home, gather firewood, get water, and cook the evening meal. At the end of the month, the co-op milk and tea checks come in the man's name. Unless you have a good man, he can do what he likes with it. It's nothing but slavery.

"Women need more say in politics, in policy making. We

need people to make noise. Somebody to see that justice is done!"

Tabitha had won me over. As we sat together and drank a cool soda in the bakery shop, I asked her more about herself. She now made her living baking *chapattis*, running her own business and selling the bread to cafeterias and restaurants. She had four half-grown children and a husband.

"My parents got mission-school educations. My mother ran away from home so that she could go to school. She became a nurse. She thought education was very important. She saw to it that I graduated from high school.

"We Kikuyu were most accepting of missionaries and education. Of course, we lost all our highlands. Other groups, like the Mau Mau, said we were traitors. But we have gone to school; we have made a lot of progress. I think we won in the end."

I liked Tabitha and treasured that unexpected hour of conversation with her. I promised myself I would go visit her soon. I would have voted for her as Minister of Children in Nairobi!

Nevertheless, I knew that to build these accidental interchanges into real friendships and relationships takes time. Trust builds slowly between those of different cultures and races.

I wanted to understand how the traditional African thought and values work. There, in the impressive downtown high rises, Western stores and restaurants, and especially in our Westlands suburb, values were eclectic. They were borrowed from wherever they seem to work. Real African life flowed somewhere else.

This was brought home to me by graphic newspaper headlines which screamed each day from page one of the *Kenya Times*. A well-known Nairobi lawyer, born into the Luo tribe, had died. Wambui Otieno, his fiery resistance-fighter wife (during the Emergency days of the 1950s when the Mau Maus rebelled against European rule) is a Kikuyu, member of a rival tribe. She wanted to bury him on their land among the Kikuyu.

Though the Otienos were educated city folks, the traditional Luos back home were incensed by this outrage to their customs. Their clan deserved the body for burial on tribal land, they argued. They deserved the inheritance as well, although everyone was careful not to bring up the money issue.

For three months the poor body was on ice in the city morgue, his spirit floating, waiting for the court's decision. Emotions ran high. According to Western law, the wife is the husband's next of kin. According to tribal law, she is no blood kin and has no say in the matter. The dead man's brothers, and then sons, would be next of kin.

The older people said, "If a wife would profit from her husband's death, it would be a terrible temptation to kill him, wouldn't it?"

While all of Nairobi waited anxiously for the verdict between Western and tribal law, more and more tribal testimony found its way onto the front pages, making us all aware of how little anyone really knows. It was oral custom, guarded by the old ones, contradicting itself and shifting ground with the witnesses.

Yet the trial was powerful evidence of the still cohesive old values of the spirit world of the ancestors, tribal survival, and loyalty by which the villages still function. In the village, the rights of the individual are sacrificed for the good of the whole group. In return, the individual is surrounded by protective relationships to save him or her from the terrors of individualism. A trade-off.

Finally the court decided that Wambui had the right to bury her husband, but she must do it on tribal land, honoring Luo custom. It was a compromise and succeeded in avoiding the threatened riots as Luos gathered in Nairobi streets outside the morgue, prepared to take the body by force if necessary. Otieno's spirit would take its place among the tribal ancestors.

It was Luo women I would be interviewing in Western Kenya, so I was eager to understand more about them. To do that, however, I needed to find my way out of the suburbs. I was in Africa, but the women I came to talk to still seemed far away.

The first unpopular family decision I made was uncharacteristically authoritarian for me. But I was adamant about it. "We're going to attend church at Eastleigh as regularly as we can," I said. Even Bob's face fell.

Don and Em lived in a corner apartment of a large neighborhood center at Eastleigh. The little congregation that straggled in there each Sunday was fluid, like most city churches, showing different faces each week.

A more charismatic Ethiopian refugee church met upstairs and sang lustily, making me wish I could speak Amharic. While these cheerful African sounds flowed through open windows and doors, we sang dismal American gospel tunes, like "When the Roll is Called Up Yonder," in slow Swahili. It was the kind of racket Eastleigh dwellers didn't notice.

Yet this little group, mostly displaced Luos who have come to the city from small congregations in the country, was struggling to coin its own identity. A few gifted young leaders were preaching and growing spiritually. Here we might at least offer some encouragement by our offering and our presence. Here I hoped to meet a few Christian sisters in a deeper way.

The family's main problem with attending this church was the hour trip it takes to get there. We rode the bus, filled on Sundays with other church-going families. The little girls wore starched ruffles, and the usual huckster women carried bags of vegetables.

We changed buses downtown, near the Hilton Hotel. On the journey out into the African Eastleigh community, we hung on to handstraps, jostled by crowds of bodies. In addition to the blare of traffic horns, Indian rock music whined sharply in minor key. We were the only white passengers, and we were roundly, stolidly stared at. I always subdued the impulse to pick my nose, finding humor in the outrageous. But Chris and Lisen agonized, balancing silent and rigid, hardly breathing, until we could fight our way off the bus.

We sometimes passed Salvation Army parades. The smiling paraders, dressed in spotless uniforms, clapped and played instruments. We passed independent churches, where members gathered under large shade trees in flowing white robes and circled some prophet who interpreted the Bible in emotional, rising tones. There were, of course, the Catholic cathedral, the large Baptist, Quaker, and Anglican churches as well. But we didn't notice them because their well-dressed worshipers preferred to conduct their religion quietly indoors.

We got off at the Eighth Avenue Mosque, where long-gowned Muslim men paced before prayers. We walked around the goats that sniffed through garbage piles and around the vegetable stand where rotten cabbage leaves littered the pavement. A half million Africans of all tribes and countries, many without official immigration papers, lived tightly packed in that section of Nairobi. They shared water taps and limited sanitation facilities. Ten people might share a room, so most living was conducted on the street, at all hours. The noise—horns, music blaring—and colorful costumes pushed our brain circuits into overload.

Yet Don and Em and their kids, Derek and DeeDee, all-Americans who love music, drama, sports, and swimming, learned to live there, to call it their "neighborhood." Here Francis, the car salesman, sang solos in his sweet tenor voice. Here Phillip, the accountant, preached, although he could not afford the bus fare to bring his wife and ten children with him each week. I knew that we could learn a lot in Eastleigh.

3. Five Women Around a Table

My instincts were right. Only weeks after we began to attend this church, I sat at a table in Eastleigh with four women from the local congregation. We ate soup Em cooked for us.

The Sunday service was over and all of us could have used a nap. But instead those four dutifully stayed to help their guest, the Westerner. They watched me with curiosity.

"Jesus chose three women to be witnesses to his resurrection," I told them.

"Jesus told them, 'Don't be afraid; go and tell what you have seen.' We owe it to each other to witness to what we have seen—to share our faith in God.

"I know Western education often discounts the wisdom of the African elders. And so our young women are tempted to lose respect for the older women. But we want to make sure that doesn't happen. We want to collect stories about the wisdom of women who truly love God. Do you want to help do this? Are there one or two women in your group who have this kind of strong faith and who would share her story with others?"

They thought for awhile. "Our group is very small," one woman apologized through our translator, Monica. "You see, we are all just ordinary people, like ourselves here. I don't know if we can help you. We have no interesting stories to tell."

We all sat in silence for a time, thinking. In Africa this was okay, I reminded myself. Silence is part of a conversation too. Finally Grace Wambui Kamau, the church elder, broke the silence. She evidently decided that here and now she would give me her own testimony and salvage the occasion. I was surprised, as I had described this as a planning meeting. But I am deeply interested in her. I did not know until later that she rarely speaks about her past.

Grace had grown stout and motherly, but she was once a pretty woman. Her eyes sparkled as if with secret laughter and she possessed a fine dry wit which was so understated one missed it at first. When she caught a joke her eyes twinkled and her lips twitched into a smile. But she did not allow herself to indulge in real laughter or other useless tomfoolery. Her mind was set on other things, invisible goals toward which, one felt, she would inexorably move. She was a determined woman.

Grace switched into Swahili to be more comfortable. Monica, a nurse, translated. Sometimes Monica got so caught up in the conversation, however, that I had to jog her elbow to remind her to keep translating.

Grace Wambui Kamau. Born 1939, Kikuyu tribe, Nairobi, Kenya.

"I have experienced how God loves me and how he has been blessing me in many ways. I will tell you my story," Mama Kamau [or Kamau's mother, as she is universally known] began with great dignity.

"I grew up in the Kikuyu highlands outside Nairobi. [This is the fertile plantation area now, set at five thousand feet altitude or higher. The bracing, healthy air is free of malaria. It has for many generations been home to industrious farming tribes.] I followed my mother's example and learned to work hard.

"In my mother's day, women were silent before men, to show respect. They made no decisions, but spent each day working from dawn to dark. They cooked breakfast, fetched water, carried their babies along to the fields, and farmed all day. On their walk home, they collected and carried loads of firewood. They brought fodder for the goats and fetched more water. They ground millet and maize into flour. At night they cooked again and each served her husband in his own living quarters. If these tasks were not done well, women were punished with beatings.

"But my parents welcomed change. My father returned from World War II with enough pay to invest in some goats. His goat business thrived, and he bought some land. Here he planted coffee for a cash crop. My mother earned money selling extra maize and potatoes in the market. They wanted me to go to school and dreamed that I could become a secretary.

"I finished all eight grades and did well. I especially enjoyed sewing, knitting—things I could do with my hands. My parents enrolled me in a business school in Nairobi, though by that time life had grown very difficult for the Kikuyu. The Emergency had begun.

"The Mau Mau rebels were terrorizing the area, trying to oust the colonials who had appropriated prize Kikuyu land for tea and coffee plantations. There was unrest for seven years.

"We couldn't travel without passbooks, soldiers, and checkpoints. Many of my relatives got hurt. It was a dangerous time. Public transportation stopped altogether. After five months of school, I had to give up. There was just no way to travel. Then I stayed home until I got married at age twenty-two.

"My husband and I found jobs in Nairobi, but city life was hard for me. I was something of a loner, and I felt uncomfortable. I met lots of people, but it was hard to make real friendships. Everyone, including me, was busy working.

"My husband tried to get me to associate with all kinds of people. But I felt this was a waste of time. At home my mother had only visited with the churchwomen.

"I worked as a housemother for the child welfare society where my husband was a warden. After work I cooked, cleaned, crocheted, and knitted. And I trained our four children, ages three, five, seven, and nine.

"Kenya had just recently won independence and under Kenyatta it seemed as if anything were possible. I guess I had my parents' drive. I planned to provide a better life for my family through sheer hard work.

"Then one day my husband left for work and never came back. Without any warning, he had abandoned his family. I was stunned. My world of hard work had caved in."

Grace's words were simple, unadorned except with a deep, deep sigh. Even now, all these years later, the wounds of that time were very deep. Her dreams, her own self-image, her security—all were shattered.

"I had two children in school and two hadn't even started yet. I was angry, hurt. My job didn't pay enough for school fees, rent, and food. I didn't know what to do! There had been no sweetness in my marriage. I was used to being lonely. But this was worse. I felt the Lord must hate me!

"Most people have a low opinion of unmarried women. They judge us to be immoral. There is a strong stigma against us. The truth is that most of us are hardworking. We try not to listen or care about what people say. We try to focus on what is going to help our children and build their futures.

"It is not easy to build a home for children. There are many, many problems. It was such hard work, and I wasn't happy. There was never enough money, and I scolded the children a lot.

"I had been brought up in a Christian home and took communion. But it hadn't been important to me. I sent the children to a nearby Sunday school, but I usually slept in on Sundays. I would hear them sing songs like *Mungu Mwema*, which means 'God is good.' And I began thinking, *God loves me? And now we are left like this, with not enough money?*

"I remembered that at the time I was baptized I was told, 'God is love.' Now I started to think about these things.

"About this time my son Kamau befriended the son of David Shenk, the director of the center at Eastleigh. My children visited back and forth and began attending Sunday school with the Shenk children. One day I decided to go with them. That day my heart was softened by the Word of God. I kept attending.

"Finally, one day in prayer, I confessed my guilt and anger to the Lord. I was saved and received Jesus as my Savior. I prayed with the pastor's family and asked the Lord to help me know how to overcome my problems.

"When one is open, the heart begins to heal. I felt my anger disappearing. Once I decided to be a follower of Christ, I found myself thinking about him and not my problems. I began to feel my salary was enough for my family. I didn't waste time or money on unnecessary things. I praised God for blessing me. I began to treat my children differently. I felt truly grateful.

"Many years have gone by now, but I still feel satisfied with the little I have. I think to myself, *My children went on with their education. I stayed well all these years and was able to feed them.* They are good children. I know I could have lost them if I hadn't followed the Word of the Lord.

"I don't dwell on my lack of a husband. Maybe all these problems I have faced have been a blessing in disguise."

Later I visited Grace repeatedly, and met her children. They are bright, stable Christians. Elizabeth Wangui, the eldest, is a mother of three and wife of an Anglican pastor. She is a secretary for New World Vision, thus fulfilling, a generation later, her grandmother's dream.

Arthur Kamau, the only son, graduated from United States colleges and is still in the United States attending graduate school. His bright sister Joyce also attends college in the United States, hoping to study law. Beatrice studies in a trade college in Nairobi.

Grace has worked since 1967 as an assistant nurse for the Nairobi City Council in a 24-bed maternity clinic. Although she works long hours and night shifts, she is eager to get back to work after vacations. She also works in her spare time, knitting items for sale on a knitting machine she paid off in installments.

She lives in a tiny apartment with sporadic electricity, shared water tap, and toilets. She cooks on a charcoal *jiko* on the floor. She puts every spare shilling she can save into her children's educations, although she earns less than $100 per month. Maybe after they are on their own she can begin saving toward a small plot of land back home and leave the crowded city. That is her dream.

"All that I have," she said, "has come from God's love. I couldn't have done this by myself."

"The Lord accepted me without a husband. So I like to think he can use me just as I am, without a husband. I read 1 Corinthians 7 when I need courage. Paul's instructions to remain single and serve the Lord have encouraged me often. I believe I am an example to others that nothing is impossible with God.

"I tell unmarried women who are building a home that it is not easy. They must first of all be near God. Unless you are close to God, how can you bring children into the light? And I tell them they must work hard. Unless you are hard-working, you simply can't do it.

"Children copy everything we do. If I'm not a succeeder, they won't succeed either. We need to take time to know what our children are thinking. They need a lot of care.

"I was called to be an elder in my congregation. I'm a Kikuyu woman in a mostly Luo group [the tribes are traditional enemies]. And I have a family of four children and no husband [also a low-status position]. To me, this shows that I was called, just as I am, as an example that God loves everyone. This could only happen because of Christian love.

"The church is my home. It is my father's house. I'd like to see our congregation move forward, to have people more lively. Satan is using divisions to keep us from moving forward. I do what I can. In the meantime, I ask the Lord to show me the way before I tackle it."

I listened intently, jotting down notes and reading body language and cues from our small group. The mood among us changed from curiosity to involvement. We were all moved by Wambui's simple, yet powerful, testimony. Evidently the other women had not known the details of what we had just heard.

I began to move toward prayer to close our meeting. But I caught a response from the shyest woman present. She wanted to speak, too. All of us invited her to begin. We made quick translation arrangements. Rosaline was Luo and Swahili was not her mother tongue, but we would have to do our best.

Rosaline Atieno Atiang. Born 1954, Luo tribe, Nairobi, Kenya.

Rosaline, 32, was a young woman with a shy but irrepressible, childlike smile. She was a newcomer to the city and talked in a gentle voice. The story flowed matter-of-factly, only her face struggling with inner emotions.

"I am a Luo, and I grew up in Tanzania as a Roman Catholic. I married a Mennonite man. To give the children a unified background, we agreed to attend the Mennonite Church together. I was welcomed into the church and I joined there at Kamageta, Kenya, where we lived.

"Three children, all girls, were born to us in 1973, 1977, and 1979. Then in 1984 tragedy struck. After ten years of marriage, my husband was killed in an auto accident. I was a housewife with no income of my own. Even before they took my husband's body away, I was asking myself, *What shall I do?"*

Rose's own father and both parents-in-law had died earlier. Aside from her mother at Shirati, Tanzania, she had no one. She knew that in Luo tradition a man who dies without a male heir leaves no issue at all. Neither Rosaline nor her daughters, as females, could inherit anything. The house, the fields, the harvest, the furniture—all belonged to the clan, her husband's brothers.

Rosaline went to her pastor and asked the anguished question, "Why did God allow this to happen?" The pastor tried to comfort her and urged her to keep praying.

But three months later, her brothers-in-law evicted Rosaline from her home, leaving her with with nothing. She had only a phone call from a Christian friend of her husband. He had found her a job if she could get to Nairobi.

"Nairobi is a terrible place," her pastor warned. "Where will you live with your children?" He knew of desperate country folks who had gone to the city with high hopes only to have unemployment, poverty, and despair break them.

But no one here wanted Rose or her little girls. So, like many others before her, she boarded a bus with them. They headed to Nairobi.

She was terrified. She arrived in the huge, traffic-clogged city at 6:00 a.m. and managed to find her way to an uncle's house. He was glad to see her. His wife was not. This was not the first poor relative who had showed up in the city, meaning to live with them awhile.

"I don't want to break up your home," Rose assured her aunt, after her uncle had left for work, the tears rolling down her cheeks. "But I don't know what to do! I was born in Tanzania, so I don't have an identity card. I'm just praying that I'll be able to get a job without it."

Three days later, Rosaline was offered the promised job as a housecleaner. No one asked for her identity card. A friend allowed her to live in a tiny kitchen where she and the three girls could sleep on the floor. She would have to work a whole month before receiving any salary, however. She was forced to borrow money, even the ten-cent bus fares, from friends. Another Christian friend kept the children while she worked. She was overjoyed.

"I cooked porridge to feed us," she murmured. "For a month we ate only porridge. And the children weren't greedy. They accepted life without complaining. That was a big help to me.

"At the end of the first month, I received my first salary. We still had very little to eat. But I put away money for school fees, so my eldest daughter could go back to school. The second month I made a school-fee payment for my second daughter. That was important to me. No matter what happened, I wanted my children to get schooling.

"I felt God had done wonders for me.

"After six months, the owner wanted her kitchen back. I looked for a place to live. But everything was expensive. I used to tell the children to kneel and pray before they slept. My older daughter would say, 'Mother we pray, but father doesn't come back.'

"My second girl would ask, 'Mother, why didn't we pray before, so that father wouldn't die?' I would tell them that everyone has to die. Once the time has come, we can't prevent it.

"But I did a lot of grieving myself. It seemed as if there was no one who could help me."

Finally Rose found a place to live. The rent was high, but she had no choice. Gradually she was able to buy a few things for housekeeping. She began worshiping with the Nairobi Mennonite Fellowship, "going there to pray." This gave her contact with the Luos from the Lake Victoria region who traveled from village to city on errands.

"In these years, I have moved nearer the Lord," she said. "I have no husband. Now Jesus can be my husband. Human beings can leave me. I don't desire another marriage now. It is better for me to stay with the Lord."

After these years as a widow, Rosaline is grateful for her blessings. She can pay for rent, food, school, and bus fare.

"My children are in school. They go to church and sing in the choir. We all like music. I think we can get by."

Rosaline still cleans houses. She has no help, no support from anyone. She lives on the edge, working hard.

"But," she said, "I have the feeling that the Lord will help me. I will stay in the heart of the Lord."

The afternoon was waning, cooling. The room in which we sat was darker. The soft light freed us to show how moved we were, we five women around the table. Somehow the city noise seemed far away. The world consisted of us, women who reached out to each other in love, listening, hearing these deep hurts and soothing them by our silence. No words were necessary.

A third woman shifted her weight. She was a country woman, with a head scarf and a kanga skirt. Her face was angular, her arms thin and muscular. As she began to speak, obviously mellowed by the other stories, she picked up an animation not apparent before.

She laughed at herself freely and spoke in a loud, quick rhythm, as though accustomed to field and market place. This made it hard for the others to follow, because she still had a country accent and was missing the six teeth that used to be knocked out as a tribal ritual. She said she cannot read or write.

"I am Ziprosah Omwalo," she began, "and I am with the Lord. If I leave the Lord, I will be left behind, and I will have nothing."

"Yes, Ziprosah has a strong faith," said Grace. "When I visit her, before we even sit down, she says, 'Now we must pray together.' "

Ziprosah told us that she grew up in Kisumu town, in Western Kenya, along Lake Victoria. At ten she was baptized as a Catholic, but when she married a second-generation Protestant, she attended church with him.

After their six children were born (two more had died), her husband brought home a second wife, against Ziprosah's will. After that, he stopped attending church. He and his new wife began drinking *pombe,* liquor. The two families still live side by side, beset by quarrels and problems.

"My husband doesn't know what we eat or wear. He is not there when we need him. It's true, he pays some of the school fee [about $60 per year] for our son, but I am responsible for food and school fees for all the rest. My brother helps me some. But it is not enough.

"There is no way to solve these problems," sighed Ziprosah.

She feels she has no recourse but to be strong and help her children survive. She lives on a meager income from buying and selling vegetables. At thirty-nine, she looks far older than her years. She worries especially about her two unmarried daughters, both of whom have children of their own. She pins her hopes on a training program in spinning and weaving her eldest daughter has entered in Eastleigh.

In the meantime, she prays. And her strong spirit allows her to laugh at herself and her troubles. And she comes, when she is not too tired and can spare time away from the market, to the Fellowship at Eastleigh, for spiritual growth. Her brother is a preacher and elder here.

"It is only because of the Lord that I was able to raise my children and feed them," she said, shaking her head. "He has given me the power and energy to work hard to care for them. There was a time when I wished my husband would die. But that doesn't help. Both he and his wife use their money for pombe. They are no help."

We all knew that it was time to go home. But we wanted to hear a word from Monica, who had worked hard at interpreting for us all afternoon. A nurse in her thirties, Monica plaited her hair tight to her head, accenting large, rolling eyes which expressed her comic streak.

She told us she was born into a non-Christian home and attended church all by herself, getting baptized at age fourteen as an Anglican. She attended Eastleigh because it was across the street from her home. Her husband was a good man but refused to accompany her to church.

"To me the name of the church doesn't matter. It is the word of God in my heart that is necessary," she said smiling.

"I've grown most at work. There we often talk about the Word of God. In the hospital we see so much. The nursing encourages faith. When I ask, 'Why did God make me like this?' I just look around and I see others' misfortunes.

"I believe that my nursing is doing something for the Lord. I don't call people 'bed number four.' I call them by name. I always think of that verse, 'If you do it to the least of these, you do it unto me.' "

Monica had four children and a stable home. She came to the center for sewing classes sometimes and had a natural curiosity about life. She was even trying out aerobics with Em. She was the statistical one woman in four with a family intact. She was happy, though hard-working, with energy left over to develop one or two of her own gifts.

We five women prayed together, mentioning each other by name, in three languages. Afterwards, reluctant to part, we promised to meet again. Grace mentioned the possibility of the Eastleigh women forming a group, which they had never done before. A vulnerability had found its way into the story-telling. We were hungry for support and love.

Mama Kamau, always the one in charge, took me with her to the bus stop, through the teeming, full ghetto streets, past the mosque, past the street peddlers. She put me safely on the number fifteen bus and waved good-bye.

There is a knack to riding a Nairobi bus which takes time to acquire. It reminded me of horseback riding on an old nag with an irregular gait. Before I found a seat, the driver popped his clutch and I flailed gracelessly for balance. An old woman grabbed my arm and pushed me into a vacant seat, her mother instinct stronger than her shyness. She and her friends chattered and grinned at the comedy of this frail white woman, at our great good fortune to have caught a bus with empty seats, and at the antics of all hilarious human beings they knew.

My head was reeling as I replayed the opened faces, the stories, the warmth of the unexpected afternoon. It was my first interview. But already I had seen a cross section of African women and their struggles.

Though this is the city, the stories of these women were the same ones I encountered everywhere for the next year in six different countries. The anger and hurt of polygamy. Desertion by men. Such legal injustices as the lack of ownership of property. The unending work women do to feed their children—these were the struggles women brought with them to God, looking for inner and outer transformations.

I was alone on a bus with strangers, with laughing African women. In a glow of solidarity with them, I too chuckled as we balanced on a rickety bus, riding a small globe careening through space. For the moment, we laughed—unafraid.

4. Lillian—A Lawyer Who Cares

In the weeks that followed I thought often of shy Rosaline, sleeping on the floor with her little girls, eating glutinous porridge in the wake of her husband's tragic death.

I knew that in tribal life women often did not inherit or own anything. Paychecks for picking tea or coffee, for example, came in the husband's name. Even the children often belonged to the father when a marriage split. When the man died, his belongings automatically went back to his clan and close relatives. Sons would later be provided for by uncles and others, when they needed help for bride-price or getting settled.

I also knew the tribe had built-in safety nets. Often a widow was offered a closely related man as a substitute for her dead husband. This guaranteed her a home and fields within the clan. Most families had some boys. They would help their mother when she got old and would gain some land within the clan as adults. But this was spare comfort to those like Rosaline who fell between the cracks. In her case, there were no levirate husbands available and no sons, no father or father-in-law to fight for her.

The fact that Rosaline was still raising children was not a good enough reason for her to inherit anything. The only way clan land and wealth would stay intact was if it stayed in the hands of the men. Women, after all, might leave the clan, marry others, and build up the families of strangers.

Men stayed and held history and tradition together. If they were not living in the village, at least they usually had a house and some family staying there most of the year. It was important, traditionally, that men hold the money.

To deny a woman the basic rights of ownership and inheritance is a shocking idea to those of us in the West. Yet only two hundred years ago, English women were in the same legal position. In those days, they were to bring a dowry with them into marriage. This money or property became the husband's. He had free legal rights to do with it what he liked.

If the woman left her husband, he retained full ownership of both dowry and children. She had no right even to visit the children without his permission. It took the French Revolution, with its rhetoric of equality and freedom, and later, the abolition of slavery, to influence feminist history. Slowly English and American women came into their own, not earning the vote until the twentieth century.

As I listened to many women during my months in Nairobi, I remembered the callous comment made by a Luo woman about a rival tribe: "If a Kikuyu wife stood to gain some inheritance from her husband's death, she would be tempted to kill him!" Of course this was not true, but it was a common prejudice reflecting some of the animosity between the two tribes.

Others hinted that it was a wife's moral job to keep her husband alive and healthy. If she failed through neglect and laziness and he died, she deserved to lose everything.

Many African women know that the traditions barring them from owning property acquired through their own work is unjust. Some consider fighting when their property is threatened.

However, there are risks to such temptations. One sixty-year-old widow, who had considered going to court to keep one field so she could continue to grow her own food, changed her mind. She decided against it for fear that relatives would curse her with witchcraft or physically hurt her.

Others feared that such rebellious acts would threaten their salvation. An older country woman added, "Suing my husband's family for my own belongings would be a sin. I'd rather go without and let God protect me!" The roomful of women present murmured agreement.

Only if the church or some upright, male relative defended them could most traditional women hope for justice.

One who had raised eight children alone after her husband's death said, "The relatives were determined to get my house and sell it. They would have succeeded if my pastor hadn't called them to a meeting and told them that my children needed to live in this house—and no one must throw me out. Pastors can really stand up for us if they want to."

She hoped that someday the church as a whole would begin preaching in favor of women's rights.

I wondered about the modern East African legal systems. How did they interpret the law? Even though women out in the country villages would not have such an opportunity, I decided to call on a Nairobi lawyer—one well respected for her advocacy of women. I wanted to find out how her story dovetailed with those of the Eastleigh women. What would she say to Rosaline, to Grace, to Ziprosah?

Lillian Mwaura. Born 1949, Kikuyu tribe, Kiambu, Kenya.

Lillian Mwaura strode out of her office, a lawyer with an aura of authority and self-confidence. She wore a dark wool suit and long, permed hair.

She glanced around the hushed waiting room, full of men who looked worried and insecure as they waited to see a lawyer. She offered me a friendly handshake. Inside her office I assured her I would not take much time. But she relaxed, shuffled legal briefs aside, and leaned back, friendly and open.

Lillian and her brother ran the private legal practice together, in the Agip Building in Nairobi. Lillian's specialty was arranging transfers, leases, legal charges, and debentures for corporations.

She volunteered time to the International Federation of Women Lawyers and served as president of the National Council of Women of Kenya. Lillian provided seminars and public education to help women know their legal rights.

"It's amazing how little they know," she sighed.

"Women are equal to men legally under our constitution," Lillian said. "The constitution is very clear that we all have equal opportunities. However, the attitudes of society change slowly. In practice, we are not yet equal. We don't yet get credit for all the roles we play in society.

"In Kenya, we apply customary laws [traditions] as long as they are not opposed or repugnant to our written law, at least in cases where one of the parties lives traditionally.

"For example, our Law of Succession Act provides for all children whom the husband was maintaining (even illegitimate ones) to receive a share of inheritance.

"Traditionally the daughters would not inherit. In this case, if one party claims tradition and the other argues for constitutional rights, a judge makes a compromise settlement or decision.

"The biggest problem is that women don't know their rights, and they don't go to court. That's how I want to help. I want to educate women.

"There is a sense of taboo about writing wills. Many men refuse to make one. But the will is necessary to protect any inheritance for wives. This is one thing we try to encourage.

"My job is very satisfying. It is not boring and keeps my mind alert. But I have to say it is very hard. You get difficult problems and difficult people to work with.

"You see, I am divorced and raising five children alone. Sometimes I feel guilty that I am so involved with my job. My brother leaves work and often goes to a club in the evening. He's free. Someone else provides for his food, clothes, and children. But me—I go home and take care of my children. I always have responsibility waiting for me.

"I am proud of my children. They are good to me. And I try to communicate with them. But sometimes, out of guilt, I try to make it up to them. Then I am afraid I spoil them."

Lillian does not plan to marry again. "I am financially independent. And I frankly don't have any leftover energy to share with someone else. I can't imagine any man could really be a father to my kids at this late date.

"Then too, I'm a Catholic. Being divorced carries a stigma. My mother had a hard time accepting it. Other people view me judgmentally. And they wouldn't accept remarriage."

Mwaura married early, entered the University of Nairobi, and gave birth to four children while she studied. Later she adopted a fifth child, a daughter. She went on to a year of law school, then internship, and became an advocate (lawyer). Her husband was also ambitious, earning a Ph.D. at Harvard. Through all this stress, the marriage crumbled.

"People trust me. But I have had to spend more time and do the job better to be considered equal to a man. My strength of character was given to me by my mother, Priscilla Waithera Mwaura. She is an amazing woman. My father died in the Emergency [years of the Mau Mau Rebellion]. She raised us so that four of us out of seven children went to the university.

"She had planted coffee early, along with other crops. On Saturdays we picked and sold coffee. The money was for education. She never stopped working. She is old but still farms.

"When I was a girl and asked for money, if it was for books my mother dredged it up. But if it was for a dress, no.

"And now I tell my kids, 'You have to work hard. The only thing I can give to you is an education. You'll have to do the rest on your own.' So in our family, education was very important.

"I've been in practice for thirteen years, and I am used to city life. But I also have a farm in Tigoni, the highlands. We have a house and some cows. On weekends we all go there, and that is my real home. That is where I belong."

5. At Home in Nairobi

By September, Chris and Lisen rode a big yellow school bus to their international school, Roslyn Academy. The new kids sat alone, pretending absorption in the scenery. The old hands, who had lived here a year or two, crowded two or three to a seat, wriggling like puppies. Parent-teacher socials, sports, musicals, and homework moved into our schedules. We Americans are skilled at taking our culture with us and recreating it anywhere!

Westlands Shopping Center was the center of our suburban life. There the children caught the bus; we mailed and received letters, bought still-warm bread for thirty cents a loaf, and hopped buses. Vendors thrust dewy, pink and red rosebuds, boxes of mulberries and strawberries, or huge, market-scene batik paintings at us. They chased us to our cars, talking nonstop while we unrolled windows to let summer heat escape.

Flower stalls were crammed with flowers of all varieties, which sold cheaply. I often splurged and bought a sprig of white tuberose for its thick, sweet smell. There were vegetable markets, of course, and old-fashioned, Indian grocery stores, with narrow, dusty aisles. There were photocopying and Kodak services, a chemist's (drugstore), a bookshop, a butcher shop, a bakery, and even a hairdresser. So life was familiar. Yet our senses were bombarded daily by the exotic and unfamiliar.

Downtown, map in hand, I found the McMillan Library and paid a weekly fee to use the books upstairs in the African Collection. In the free downstairs reading room, crowds of young black students vied for seats to read current newspapers and periodicals. It was lighted, a good place to study.

Upstairs there was no one but me. There the books were dusty, old, seldom used. Nevertheless, I took notes, added them to my growing lists of statistics. I wrote the following in my notebook:

- Kenya. Tiny. Size of New York (state). Twenty-three million population.
- Universal popularity with world travelers. It boasts more human, animal, and environmental variety within its borders than most continents do.
- From the dusty, almost naked nomads of North; to the ambitious Kikuyu farmers of the fertile highlands; to the tall, red-robed Maasai who remind us of an ancient, noble civilization, tribal uniqueness is fascinating.
- "Kenya is a damned zoo. Everybody rides around in buses

painted in zebra stripes, staring at the people and the animals."—United Nations official I met on a plane.

- Kenyans deal with constant infiltration from India and the West. One hundred thousand expatriates live in Nairobi alone. Eight hundred non-governmental agencies registered here. Kenyans are a strange mix of African and Western values, and the balance shifts from day to day.
- It is easy to recognize social injustice here. There is a big gap between rich and poor. But people flock here for good hospitals, schools, westernization.
- Young Kenyans wear jeans, sneakers, T-shirts. Love rock music. Have romantic notions about marriage.
- Their grandparents often still live in villages. Believe in the spirit world, old cohesive tribal ties and values, polygamy, authority of the old.
- Westerners are fearful about Kenya's overpopulation. Half its people are under twenty-one years. Four per cent growth rate per year is world's highest. In thirty years population will rise from twenty-three million to seventy-nine million people.
- Fertile lands are already filled with people who farm every available inch. A huge population influx will outstrip the country's ability to provide housing, food, and fuel. Wood provides 90 per cent of country's cooking fuel. Kenya cannot afford to lose any more trees as it fights erosion and overgrazing in marginal, semiarid land.
- Cities are already overtaxed, with massive unemployment and long waiting lists for elementary schools. There are few social services for the old or disabled. Families care for these members. But in the cities, these ties break down.
- The national health system is overtaxed. In outlying areas patients lie two abed in hospitals, often with no sheets. At Thika District Hospital, some six hundred patients occupy space meant for two hundred. The morgue has eight freezers but receives fifty bodies a day. "The smell of rotting bodies has spread to the hospital kitchen." The government says it lacks funds.
- Kenyans themselves are lukewarm to birth control. They are

still optimistic about their country's prospects. Men are proud of large families as evidence of virility. One man, Dinja, of Nyanza, boasts he has fathered 497 children. Most men are content with ten or so.

- Women, too, earn social security and personal fulfillment through their children. There are few other avenues.
- Kenyans are proud of their country. They see expatriates flooding in, exclaiming over the beauty. They know Kenya is a good place.
- Kenya has a remarkably stable government. A one party system, with no real opposition allowed. Africans feel they cannot afford the financial waste and unsettling psychology of the West's two-party system and public wrangling.
- Newspapers may publish only mild criticism of government. People speak carefully about politics, fearing detention.
- The country is largely Christian, with Moslem and animist minorities. Churches are full and overflowing. Here ordinary people learn participatory democracy and order their lives around strong moral values.
- In churches the same political problems rear heads as in government. Leaders begin well, then degenerate into morasses of tribal loyalties and family obligations to relatives. When new leaders rise in protest, the old ones turn unexpectedly autocratic and squelch them mercilessly. Strong ties, first to the clan and then to the tribe, are deeply embedded.
- For young Christians, exhilaration to become part of a new, inclusive tribe that transcends the old loyalties. But the realities of tribal values are there to complicate congregational life and to tangle up its leaders.
- Yet Kenyans do not give up their faith. They say the devil is a real opponent who roams the spirit world to defeat them. They throw themselves on God's mercy with a surety Westerners envy. They grieve for the spiritual arrogance they see in so many Westerners.

CHAPTER

The Evangelists

1. Kisumu, Western Kenya

For four weeks Bob, Chris, Lisen, and I walked and rode buses, feeling naked and exposed as people stared at us. I wanted to write a book titled *White Like Me.* As we dodged through black crowds in markets and streets, we became used to hearing the darting word *wazungu,* meaning white Europeans or foreigners, much as blacks must once have heard the hiss, "Niggers." Somehow, that word penetrated through thick walls of chatter and traffic din and pricked us. It was usually accompanied, not by hostility, but by curious open stares, as people stopped to watch us.

Now, however, we were gratefully encapsulated in a rented Datsun, picking our way out of Nairobi traffic American-style. Safely behind glass we felt free, safe, able to process the thousands of impressions that bombarded us since we arrived a month ago. We stared back now through the glass, like other tourists, without remorse.

We left the city behind, heading northwest on the single highway that ribbons across Kenya east-west. Here in the high country we passed coffee and tea plantations. We drove through green hills terraced in intensely cultivated *shambas* or gardens.

Along the highway, farmers displayed baskets of cabbages, potatoes, beans, tomatoes, and oranges for sale. Little boys held up live rabbits by the feet or bundles of rhubarb. Sheepskins were stretched on pole racks for sale. We stopped and bargained for a length of sugarcane that three young boys chopped up for us. My maternal instincts cringed at the fast little hands and the whack of the machete. Three shillings, eighteen cents. Lisen and

Chris spent the next hour chewing and gnawing, spitting the woody fiber out the window after they got the sweet juice.

Bob and I marveled as we absorbed what unfolded before us. To us newcomers, it was always a surprise to see these pliant people sitting astride two cultures without losing their balance. We had never, except through books, known a culture other than our own. Now we met country folks who spoke three languages and had always been exposed to neighboring tribes, foreigners, and strange customs. For many groups, survival itself meant keeping a grip on their land, language, and traditions while processing the new.

A barefoot herdsboy leading two goats walked along the road, undulating to the music of a large box-style radio. Several men in Western suits pushed a heavy wooden cart uphill on the highway, lacking a mule to do it for them. A Kikuyu woman, carrying strap around her forehead, bent low under a seventy-pound load of firewood, oblivious to traffic zooming by her at seventy kilometers per hour. A businessman with his attache case stepped off a bus and paused to urinate before he walked home, his back turned politely to the others at the bus stop.

The *matatus* (vans), which offered eighteen-cent rides, bulged with cargo and people, all moving—to market, home again—but busy earning today's shillings. People on foot streamed in constant traffic beside the highway.

Beyond the highway, the matatus, and the heavy pedestrian traffic, we saw handsome oxen plowing fertile land. The small mud-and-thatch-roofed houses were surrounded neatly with bananas, sugar cane, cassava, and maize. Women and their many children bent to weed spotless gardens. The boys spent long days herding a few cows or goats along roadsides or wherever fresh grass appeared.

For some crazy reason, it reminded me of Lancaster County, Pennsylvania. I thought fondly of the Amish back home and their deep respect for tradition, for children, for the land. They would have fitted right in. In fact, Tanzanian development workers later told us they would give anything for some Amish volunteers. They needed people who knew something about efficient harnesses, farming without machinery—people respect-

Callslip Request 4/30/2015 6:19:59 PM

Request date:4/30/2015 11:44 AM
Request ID: 49520
Call Number:305.42 C971
Item Barcode: 34711001284225
Author: Cummings, Mary Lou
Title: Surviving without romance : African wom
Enumeration:c.1Year:
Patron Name:Eunhye Chang
Patron Barcode: 522445

Patron comment:

Request number: 49520

Route to:
I-Share Library:

Library Pick Up Location:

ful of tradition and a slower pace.

The highway wound along the Rift Valley, with Lakes Naivasha and then Nakuru below and to our left. Nakuru lay in the distance. Its soft gray water was studded with tiny pink gems pearled around the edge; we knew they were thousands of flamingos.

Lake Nakuru was one of our favorite places in Kenya, but there was no time to stop that day. A shallow soda lake, its peculiar alkalinity nurtures an algae that feeds a small fish the flamingos eat. Thousands and thousands of the greater and lesser flamingos, both pink and white, crowd the edges of the lake, propped on one thin leg, scooping the water for dinner.

Cormorants, pelicans, and waterbirds of all types also congregate there. One was deafened by the great, unpleasant squawking and din of the birds. The shore smelled like my grandfather's long-defunct chicken farm. All of a sudden a bird somewhere rose in alarm. Then there was a quick swoop as some cohesive element known only to themselves moved like electricity, and hundreds of pink birds rose in unison, suddenly quiet and graceful, a long line rising into the white clouds.

Reluctantly we drove on, then we dropped, crossed the desert-like Rift Valley, climbed again on the other side, to more farmland. We continued westward, until by late afternoon we dropped again to the flat, dry country around Lake Victoria. This was Luo land, our destination, some 700 kilometers from the coast and 350 kilometers from Nairobi.

We were all hot and dusty and dry by now, even though we had stopped for warm sodas and carried our own water. We headed for a colonial English-style hotel in downtown Kisumu, the third largest town in Kenya. Here the four of us settled gratefully for two sagging beds.

But the grillwork annoyed us. It was open from floor to knee-height. This allowed our noise to be heard clearly in the open hall. And it brought in the outdoor traffic noises of trucks without mufflers gunning their motors on the street. Surprisingly, many of the tapes we made in Africa were laced, not with the sound of birds and wildlife, but with the din of trucks revving old engines without mufflers.

On Saturday we headed out of town, according to our directions, and turned off the highway onto an unmarked track. We lurched through the ruts past several Luo villages and turned up an unmarked lane. We found a charming, white, country church, complete with bell tower and shade trees—the Kisumu Mennonite Church, of typical missionary vintage.

It was empty, and we looked inside. Simple, slatted benches, a platform and altar, cement floor. A drum, tambourine, rattle, one-string harp, and a Swahili Bible lay scattered on empty benches. Someone had been teaching church history in Reformation times. On a blackboard at the back, some left-over notes in Luo: Felix Manz, Conrad Grebel, George Blaurock, Menno Simons, priesthood of believers, adult baptism, persecution.

It was Sunday morning. All of us were nervous. Pastor Musa Adongo, with whom we visited yesterday and whose dignified style and warmth we admired, asked us to wait outside. The congregation of fifty or so warmed up with lively African choruses.

Then we were paraded in, behind pastor Musa and another young leader. We sat up front, in clear view of the congregation. Lisen and Chris made surreptitious faces at each other and tried to stay sober. Bob and I occasionally glanced at the church people and always found them examining us back. It was our first visit in a country church, and we were on our own.

I worried because mine was the only woman's head not covered. Bob was sweating. He had been asked to preach. But as the service continued, we relaxed. Some hymns. Announcements. Report of a seminar. Sermon. Prayer. Familiar and reassuring elements of worship.

Pastor Musa, in his late sixties, a tall, dignified patriarch of the church, had just returned from a conference on AIDS. He taught his congregation firmly and directly about AIDS, how it is contracted and avoided. Then the mamas, women of fifty and over, jumped up. They clapped a rhythm, and led out in traditional song. These feisty women were at an uninhibited age and free to be themselves at last.

Younger Luo women, discreetly nursing the babies that were never put down, were far more shy and demure, especially when men or strangers were present. They presented no opinions and hardly spoke, even when spoken to. When the door shut on the men, however, these women raised drill-sergeant voices to their children and chattered and laughed with zest.

I had the impression that here in Luo land the two sexes maintained elaborate pretenses which no one believed for a minute—but which all believed should be preserved. They weren't quite sure what to do with a Western woman who had the bad habit of speaking up loudly in mixed company. So at the table, for example, they usually placed me with the men.

I accepted this meekly. The interpreters in mixed company were usually men, and the prospect of eating alone with the women when none of us could speak to each other was just too intimidating. And by the time the chicken was killed and we got around to eating, I was usually starved. I didn't relish waiting for the men to finish as the other women did. I soothed my conscience by assuming, or at least hoping, that the women swiped tidbits from the pots as they cooked.

The younger women, the demure ones, and the men had a second choir. This one was more modern than the mamas' music. The harmonies were almost Motown in sound, and the music was choreographed with gentle swaying hand and body movement. The hymns we sang together were old gospel songs like "When the Roll is Called Up Yonder," or "What a Friend We Have in Jesus," sung in Swahili. Since this is a phonetic language we all sang along, reading easily.

After church, people were friendly, despite the language barrier. Rosa, a beautiful young woman, showed me a list on the door: who will clean, who will lead music, who will preach. Obviously this group felt total ownership of their congregation and deep loyalty to it.

There were no written Sunday school materials, pictures, or paper and pencils for the children. I saw few Swahili stories or pictures for black children other than in the largest mission churches. These small churches operated with their Bibles and hymn books. Choir music was important and learned from visiting choirs by ear, by rote.

This was our first experience of worship in rural Kenya but wouldn't be our last. Most churches were small because all the people must live within walking distance. In the mission settlements, where there were also hospitals, schools, and missionary houses, one often found huge town churches. Five hundred people might worship on Sundays, complete with four or five choirs.

These churches were similar, just smaller, with tin roofs, no electric lights, white walls, cement floors, and slatted benches. Farther out in the country, churches were made with home-burned bricks and donated tin roofs, looking much more African. But everywhere we found local leadership, not missionaries, running the churches.

Bob and I put out feelers on this trip, trying to find local interest and leadership for the story-gathering project. We began with the pastors, most of whom were warm and helpful and referred us to the women's groups. Women were excluded from most denominational decision making and committee work. At the local level, however, they served as elders or church council members, song leaders, evangelists, and did pastoral ministry among the women.

Now we were excited to find that they were indeed enthusiastic about this project. The women stayed cheerfully after church, even though it was already 1:00 p.m., they had had no lunch, and they still had a long walk home in the sun.

Of course, they had stories to tell, almost all of them had stories to tell. And, yes, they would all help me. What a miracle it is, they said, to have a stranger come along who is interested in encouraging women in their faith. It is rare, they said, that anyone shows any interest in women.

On this same morning, I met a wonderful woman, home visiting for the holidays, who translated for me with sparkle and zest. A young mother and teacher, Rebecca Osiro became my mainstay in Kenya for the rest of the year. I praised God that at each new venture God provided me with a person like Rebecca.

It was increasingly obvious that I would be the motivator, getting things moving, encouraging people. But local leaders would need to be deeply involved for this project to work. And here was Rebecca, brimming with intelligence and talent, already excited about this new opportunity for women like her mother, who have been so often overlooked. Rebecca and women like her in each town formed the bridge of understanding between my world and the village world.

And it was with Rebecca that I went back to Kisumu several months later to begin collecting stories. Together we probed to find women who were pioneers in building the African church.

"You know," Rebecca told me, "some of these women are so dramatic—they have such good stories to tell. But there are others, too, the quiet ones, who have been the quiet strength.

"Some of them are married to church leaders. And those leaders may have done some backsliding. In some cases, it is those women who were loving and patient, and brought those leaders back to the Lord. They are the real Christians."

She was right. There were so many unsung heroes among the women. They are the real strength of the African church. Among themselves, without status or title, they pray with the sick, sit up all night, and sing with the bereaved. They comfort each other, pray together, and preach from favorite Bible passages to each other. Without fanfare they forgive husbands and family members who have wronged them. Thus, they bring reconciliation to the whole family.

To an American woman, afraid to pray with someone who was suffering, afraid it might be presumptuous, it was liberating to see women who were so confident in their faith and so free to share it. Simple African women, without education or status, felt free to pray for, to bless, and to preach to me, a stranger, without apology or motive. It was a moving and humbling experience.

The following stories tell of several women called to work as leaders in the African church. In some way, each had received a sense of God's call, though never an ordination. I have purposely selected two age generations, as well as both city and country women with widely diversified education and gifts. These women are symbolic of the many called by God to serve the African church, each in her own way. There are many others who imitate Christ and radiate his love in ways known only to their own villages.

2. Rosabella—We Were the Pioneers

Rosabella Achieng Migire. Born 1916, Luo tribe, Kadem, Kenya. Lives in Mikondo, Tanzania.

Sometimes gregarious African Christians gathered around one of my scheduled interviews and turned it into an event. These unscheduled parties threw monkey wrenches into my interview plans, leaving me little time to spend alone with the women I had come to see. Nevertheless, they provided some of my warmest memories.

One such event was at Mikondo. The bishop's young wife, Margaret, offered to drive us to Mikondo, a village about seven miles from Shirati, in the bishop's car. She made all the arrangements for Gloria Bontrager and me. She told us little about the woman I would interview there.

Gloria was our hostess in Shirati. We discovered to our delight that we came from the same hometown and high school back in Pennsylvania, although I only knew her older sisters.

She was doing home schooling with her two youngest children. Bob sometimes took that job over for all the children, so that she could accompany me; our children planned sleepovers and played like cousins. It was a pleasure to see her rapport with local women. I learned a lot by watching her.

As usual, our van was filled with an assortment of people from Shirati who needed transportation. Some we dropped off on the way; others were women relatives who were needed to help with cooking. Some of these were second wives of Christian men who should not have strayed, and a vague air of polite embarrassment hung over them. I did not inquire into matters too deeply.

At Mikondo we pulled up outside a very large, pleasant concrete house, surrounded by prosperous fields and corrals. The green of healthy maize and millet stretched around us. Faint lavender hills beyond seemed to protect the fields. This was the home of the old deacon and his wife, Zaphaniah and Rosabella Migire.

The old man was tall, gracious, and gentle. His wife was massive, her face sculpted from sterner stuff. They carried the air of patriarch and matriarch, of gentle royalty. When I took their photograph, he reached out and took his wife's hand, the only such gesture I saw in all East Africa. In his other hand, he held a Bible.

Word of our arrival spread and a group from the local congregation soon assembled. There was a meeting, during which I told them the story of a woman from Zaire. My assurance that, not only Zairians but also Americans, have problems they must take to the Lord intrigued the young people.

"What are your problems?" they asked. "What do you do about teenage pregnancies? Do your young people use liquor and drugs like ours do? How does the American church handle divorce? What happens to the children in case of a divorce?"

A magnificent meal was served. Beef, chicken, fish, ugali, rice, and sweet tea for dessert. I was surprised to see, again for the first time, that everyone was being served together. Men and women alike crowded around two improvised tables.

"You see this," noted one especially articulate young man named Gilliom. "In the old days, the women and children would have been sent away to eat together. But we don't treat women as second-class people anymore!"

Another young person asked whether women should be preaching. One man at our table stayed silent. A second laughed, obviously threatened, and quoted St. Paul.

Gilliom jumped in. "We are getting close to the end times," he said seriously. "In the end times, the Holy Spirit will manifest itself in new and powerful ways. This will come through women, through uneducated people—the words are God's, not their own. We must agree not to stifle the Holy Spirit!"

The Migires were an unusual family. Although they represented the first generation of Christians in Tanzania, they were also progressive old people. There was real openness around these tables. Together they had helped start eight small congregations in this area in the last fifty years. They were obviously well loved.

Finally I was able to spirit Mama Rosabella away from the larger crowd. We carried chairs to the edge of the yard under a shade tree. She told her story to Gloria, the local missionary, and me.

"When I was a young wife, in 1934, we moved to Shirati. There my husband and I joined some others who worshiped under a tree. I saw that these were good people. I wanted to be a person of God, like them. My husband was baptized first. Shortly afterward I was baptized, too.

"My husband was one of those men chosen to study the Bible. We were very happy about it. There was a new school at Bukiroba, a two-day journey by foot, and he was invited to go there to study. We set out, carrying all our food and belongings, with a month-old baby and a small child. It was a hard journey! But we wanted to go on learning to be people of God.

"When we arrived at Bukiroba, we had no fields and needed to make a living. The missionaries agreed to pay us four shillings, a day's flour, and a handful of meat each day. In return, we six women worked from seven to twelve o'clock each morning while the men studied. In the afternoon, the men worked.

"We women carried heavy rocks down a nearby mountain to the mission. They were going to use the rocks for the first buildings there. I couldn't carry rocks *and* my newborn baby, so I tied him on the back of my five-year-old child. The child walked with me up and down the mountain so that I could watch them both while I carried rocks.

"Oh, we worked hard! After the rocks, we carried ground in big *debbes* on our heads.

"But those were such good years. The friends we made at Bukiroba have been our good friends ever since. Many of those people have already died. The others are waiting to go to God. Together we built the church here in Tanzania. We were the foundation.

"Sometimes I would accompany two women missionaries on evangelistic visits to other villages. We would walk fifteen miles on foot, carrying our food with us. We didn't want to be a burden to the women we visited, so we would bring our own food and cook together. We would visit in homes and then gather lots of people for a service on Sunday. The women felt great joy in our visits."

Rosabella chuckled as she remembered some of their adventures on those trips: the time she stepped behind a bush to relieve herself and fell into a swamp; the time the missionary dropped Rosabella's baby in the dark; the boats they sometimes boarded on the lake, struggling up and down treacherous ladders with their babies.

"Two times a year the women and girls would walk [fifteen to twenty miles] to district church meetings in Migori or Kamageta. Oh yes, I used to walk great distances, but I can't do it anymore."

Mama Migire's face was dark. Sunlight through the leaves played on her face, making dramatic light planes. Her voice was almost a man's voice, her chuckle soft, as she remembered her youth before her massive flesh made her a prisoner of her weak legs.

"After two years at Bukiroba, I gave birth to my third living child. Then I became very sick. I was in so much pain I didn't even know I'd had a baby. The missionaries took that baby and cared for it for three months! I really loved them for that. We were all working together for the Lord.

"Because of my health, my husband left the school and we returned to Shirati. He became a primary school teacher there and also spent a lot of time as an evangelist. We helped start three churches: Tatwe, Busurwa, and Mikondo. We also spent many weekends visiting other communities and helping church planters there.

"Thirteen children were born to us. Four sons and five daughters are still living. I raised large fields to feed my family. Now my grown sons help, and they use oxen to plow. We have a good *shamba* here. Sometimes now we have eight or nine storage bins full of maize and millet after harvest!

"My husband and I tithe our cows and our crops. God gave it to us, and we return it to God. We often donate a cow for district church events. We give perhaps twenty cows to people who are in need or have problems. God has been good!

"Migire was appointed deacon at Mikondo District and we have worked hard here. There are now eight churches in the district. They are alive and growing. My husband always encouraged me to go out on three- to four-day evangelistic visits with the women. He went out at other times with the men.

"My husband and I are getting old. But even if we are taken

away now, there are many coming behind us to carry on God's work—people like those gathered in my house today.

"I work as an elder for the women. I speak up for the women of the church. I also am the person for hospitality. I have a large house right near the church, so people naturally gather here.

"We feel the respect of the young people here. Many people walked to Shirati, a thirteen-mile round trip, to visit my husband when he was in the hospital. People quickly carry a chair for me since my legs are so bad. They show us love.

"Our children are Christians. They respect us, too. God did a great thing in our house. We stayed, just the two of us, my husband and I. Many other men took more wives, but Migire always lived in a straight line. Even his family was afraid to suggest more wives because they saw this. We always prayed to God. That is what kept us together. We worked together for God.

"Two of our sons got college educations in the United States. Although we still pray together, they left the church because they took more wives. There is a lot of social pressure here to do that.

"The family is so important. Parents should pray for their children when they get married. They can encourage their children to pray their way through their troubles. Let them know they can get past their problems.

"For those starting out in their life in Christ, I would say, 'Put God first in your life. Look out for the children, orphans, and the poor. Don't do evil for evil, but do good and God will bless you.'

"Husbands will see and even become Christians this way. If a woman has the courage to talk about her faith, the husband will begin to see—to understand.

"I think it is easier for women to be Christians. We are closer to our spirits than men are. So it is easier to come to God's presence, to ask for help. Many men are impatient. They want to be the head of the house, important. They are too proud to put themselves under God.

"I've been very sick. I had an appendectomy at Mwanza, earlier this year. Terrible infections followed. In all, I had four operations. But I wasn't afraid. I was comforted by John 14:1-2. "Let not your hearts be troubled; believe in God, believe also in me.

In my Father's house are many rooms; if it were not so, would I have told you that I go to prepare a place for you?"

3. Rosalida—Survivor of a Maasai Attack

Rosalida Ong'alla. Born 1929, Luo-Kajulu tribe, Kisumu, Kenya.

Jackton Ong'alla left Tanzania and returned home to Kenya to marry a hometown girl. He came back a year later with this tall, thin Luo girl with fire in her eye and a baby on her back already. She was something of a bully, not afraid of anything, people said. She would even waylay women on their way to church or market and refuse to let them pass until they had given her some of their bananas. But she was only fourteen, still young. Her name was Rosalida, and she not only knew how to read but was wiry and strong.

Her mother-in-law soon set Rosalida to work and taught her how to brew pombe, a good local money-maker. Soon she became known for her excellent brew. Jackton was not tempted to drink elsewhere because Rosalida made the best.

One day Rosalida finished a big pot of pombe and called her older brother-in-law and some friends to come. The men enjoyed sipping from the pot through long straws as they leaned against the walls of the house. After two of the older men were drunk, they began fighting. Finally a relative stripped off his clothes and ran naked through the village.

"Look what you've done," a friend scolded Rosalida. "This relative has shamed himself forever, all because of your pombe."

Jackton and Rosalida were horrified at what had occurred. They decided they would attend the local church. Jackton also stopped drinking.

In 1951 the Ong'allas joined the church. Jackton was a quiet person, but Rosalida had a fiery personality and threw herself into her new religion. The following year she was selected for a local school committee. In 1953 she became a local and regional church leader.

One Saturday night Rosalida had dreamed that she was gathering with others from the church. All of them were studying their Bibles, and several were preaching. The next morning at church, the elders invited her to preach that very morning. She was afraid. She had never done anything like that before. But she remembered her dream, took courage, and tried. The people accepted her readily, and her confidence soared.

"God called me to preach and to sing. I am usually chosen to lead the singing, too. I don't understand why, myself, because it is very unusual for a Luo woman to be asked to preach. Later they said to me, 'Feel free to go behind the pulpit.' I know God called me to do it," Rosalida said.

"My life was much happier after that. I especially preached to those who were drinking and helped them not to backslide. I could see the fruits. I knew what that was all about; they couldn't fool me. At first after I stopped brewing I thought I'd have financial problems. But later, when I preached, I was often given a fraction of the offering. And we did not suffer for food.

There was suffering, however. Three of Rosalida's babies died in the first months of their lives. A fifteen-year-old daughter also became suddenly ill, then unconscious. She came back to consciousness and began to talk, prophesying various things about people she knew. She told people about their sins, and they repented. After several hours she died. Her death shook the whole village.

Some years later, Rosalida's seventeen-year-old daughter came home from school. She was pregnant by a married teacher. The family was irate and decided to follow custom. They found an old man, one of the father's friends, who would marry her out of friendship for the family, even though he was not eager to do it.

One day a group of teachers from the school came to visit her. They sat laughing and talking. Later her brother scolded her. "Are you still intent on shaming the family? You must never talk to that teacher again!"

That night Rosalida preached about death at the funeral of a child. She spent the night sitting with the bereaved parents. When she arrived home next morning, her own daughter was dead. She had poisoned herself.

"Oh, that was hard for me," she says softly. "I saw God's revelation to me. I needed to understand the truth, not just voice words. I needed God's strength to survive that. Later we decided to leave Tanzania, to get away from the sadness. We had lost five children, and we had two living sons and three daughters."

A whole group of Luos migrated to Ogwedhi, Kenya, to Maasai territory. Although there was a shortage of good farmland in Kenya, the Maasai had traditionally used this land only for grazing. But the Maasai were friendly and gave the Luos a piece of land to settle on.

The industrious Luos built small houses and began to farm. Rosalida again became a leader. She began a small church which met in a thatched house. Soon those of other denominations joined in.

"Why don't you bring in some of your church leaders," they suggested, "and ask them to put up a better church for us?"

"Well, I'll invite them," she said. "But I think we can build our own church. We can begin by cutting poles and thatch."

On the appointed day, a group of Luos left home to cut poles for the new church. While they were gone, the Maasai *morans*, young warriors who disagreed with their more peaceful elders, attacked the Luo village. They killed twenty people and burned everything.

The Ong'allas ran for their lives to the nearest police station. Behind them burned their house, small church, clothes, and twelve sacks of maize. They had no money, food, home, or clothes, but at least they were alive.

The police did not know what to do; they packed up the remaining Luos on a truck and drove them, hungry and thirsty, back to the Kisumu area, their homeland. They dropped them off at the big market. The Luos were still dirty from the work they had been doing during the attack.

The Ong'allas had fifty shillings ($3.00) that missionaries had given them to feed the children and a big *sufuria* (pot).

Word spread quickly. Christians gathered money and came to offer their help and support. The money was enough for a tiny piece of land. The church helped the Ong'allas build a two-room mud-walled, tin-roofed home, which is still their home today.

The Maasai attack occurred in 1975. Rosalida has still not replaced her eyeglasses or her Luo-language Bible, both lost then. She shrugged. "Neither of us ever earned more than twenty shillings [$1.25] at one time."

One beautiful result of the Ogwedhi massacre, however, was that the Maasai elders and the Mennonite Luos sat together. They discussed how to make things right between them. They decided to sponsor a peace project to help both tribes, and the Ogwedhi project was born. A school, model agricultural project, and church have helped hundreds of people improve their lives in this undeveloped corner of Kenya.

Back in her home area, Rosalida found that it was natural to minister to other Tanzanian Luos who had moved from place to place. She walked about five miles to the Obwalo church each week.

During one rainy season, the river she had to cross flooded. As she waded across, she lost her balance and got swept away. That scared her. But she still attended each Sunday. On Thursdays she joined the others in visiting homes.

Finally Pastor Musa Adongo suggested she should start her own church so she would not have to walk. "If God gives you two or three believers, then you should begin a new church," he told her.

That same night two men visited her home. They said they were fed up with their own church and would help her build a church. Gradually a group formed. They built themselves a church building and named it Alara Mennonite Church.

At the same time, Rosalida and two men formed a team to visit scattered Tanzanian Luos and pray with them. From this ministry, two more house churches began.

In later years, Rosalida walked to the area beyond the nearby mountains to visit and pray with people. Since this was a four-hour walk, she went on Saturday. Then on Sunday, after visiting individual homes, she gathered a group for a worship service. In the afternoon she walked home again.

She is getting older now and has been asked to come and start a sixth church in a new area. She would like to do it if she lives long enough.

Rosalida thinks of herself as an evangelist. When I asked her for a philosophy of evangelism she said, "I am friendly by nature, so I enjoy visiting people. I pray with them, and I ask if they are going to church. Many times people are not going. So I ask them to go to any church, I don't care which one. I visit often, maybe three or four times.

"One woman asked me to come visit her because she was having trouble with her husband. So I went. The husband was drunk and chased me with a spear. I ran for my life! But I made sure I visited often after that. He was trying to frighten me, not kill me. I understand how it is with people who drink.

"That woman was so impressed with our church. You see, we contribute to a burial, sit all night with the bereaved, visit the sick. She wanted to find a place where she could be accepted for what she was. She was eventually instrumental in starting her own church.

"When I visit, I take maize and beans with me to share with people who drop in to hear the Word. My sons work on nearby farms for a living; sometimes they give me some paraffin or firewood which I take along when I stay up all night with the bereaved. When someone is sick, I often fetch water, bathe the sick, or prepare food.

"My favorite verse has always been from the story Jesus tells about the Son of man on his throne. The righteous ask:

> And when did we see thee sick or in prison and visit thee? And the King will answer them, "Truly, I say to you, as you did it to one of the least of these my brethren, you did it unto me" [Matthew 25:39-40].

"I always wanted to help people when I could. I do not have the heart for them to become Mennonite. I just want them to find God.

"To those who follow me in this work I have this advice: Problems should not set you back. Keep preaching. Don't force anyone, just be friendly and visit frequently.

"For women who have problems with their husbands, I say, 'Don't disobey. Give your husband even more respect and love.

This often helps husbands to set their wives free to participate more in the church.'

"My own husband has been so helpful. If I stay away from home for three days, he prepares the food. When other men urge him to chastise me and keep me at home doing housework, he always says, 'If God chose her to do the work, let her do it!'

"One time the head of our clan had the police pick me up. He accused me of loitering around, not working. But my husband defended me.

"I come home from my trips, and I work hard. But after several days I get the call to go out again. I am restless. I don't get tired doing the Lord's work."

I remember Rosalida, dressed rather poorly, standing erect and dignified in a women's meeting, her low voice raised in charismatic, fervent prayer. There was no doubt this country evangelist, traveling on foot, without church office or status, was giving the little she had to the Lord.

4. Lois—A Twin Who Didn't Get Thrown Away

Lois Kiangwe Buteng'e. Born 1941, Mkuria tribe, Mugongo, Tanzania.

Although the town boasted a new Western-staffed hospital, its aura was Dodge City, 1860. Huge potholes and gullies pocked the town's main, dirt road. Dry dust eddied as the wind lifted it. Scarred Land Rovers nuzzled the board steps of shabby storefronts, waiting for five-minute shoppers. There was not much to buy except the basic supplies—cooking oil, beans, maize flour, tea, imported tinned foods, kerosene, and matches.

Mugumu was the center of government for the Serengeti District, an area sparsely populated, largely given over to the huge Serengeti National Game Park. These were grasslands. Rolling hills were dotted with thorn trees. Stands of trees with thick foliage lined only the rivers, which narrowed at this time of year.

Tom (a United States doctor), Jill, and their two small girls lived in an attractive house next to the hospital, their walls hung with good-quality African art. Both adults were still recovering from a severe bout of hepatitis. They were weak and discouraged. Out here they didn't receive much moral support from other Westerners. The needs of the hospital were so intense Tom could hardly leave, but Jill was excited about today's outing.

Jan Bender Shetler was the experienced Westerner among us, although her home was several hours' drive away. We leaned on her. She had brought her baby along as usual. In true African style, he was held, nursed, and passed around constantly.

Jan was a community development worker, along with her husband. Their role was to encourage local congregations wanting to start a project such as installing a local hammermill for grinding grain or setting up a carpentry shop to train its young men. They did much legwork, learned to ask questions, and found out whom to contact to solve problems. Then they brought back options to the local leaders.

Jill, Jan, and I climbed into the battered four-wheel-drive Land Rover with Ludia, the national church leader who would conduct the interview with us and translate. Jan took off. We tilted precariously as she ground out of the gullies that gashed the dirt road, even in the center of town. She had decided that driving at forty mph and "taking your lumps" is not much more painful than crawling through them at fifteen mph. My head cracked into the ceiling as the Land Rover dropped suddenly and then rose with a vicious jerk to the left.

We passed the local church, three-fourths finished. Parishioners, mostly women, made their own mud bricks, adding sand from the ancient high termite mounds for strength. The bricks were burned in round, homemade, mud kilns and then were set with mud plaster. Usually the denomination provided the expensive tin roof and perhaps the cement floor.

The local people were proud of their church, called Morotonga. They were already busy with other self-help projects, encouraged by Pete and Jan.

We pulled up outside a tin-roofed home. It had a few trees in the dirt yard, giving it a distinct European look. It was the pastor's house. Several young women were already assembling at the backyard kitchen, a lean-to shaded by palm branches. The young women did the cooking at church events. The middle-aged and older women sat back and enjoyed themselves.

Lois Kiangwe greeted us warmly and took us inside. She seated us on a black plastic settee and chairs covered with the crocheted doilies we saw everywhere. Then she disappeared in a flurry. There were whispered conferences outside the door. Young children wandered in to look at us, lost interest, and ran out. Chickens squawked in the yard. I supposed that one chicken had lost his head. Lois dashed in, a whirlwind, and swept children and furniture into place. She ran out again. We heard her laugh as she greeted another friend who had come for the occasion.

Lois was small-boned and pretty. She was in her late forties but looked ten years younger. She wore a cheerful red head scarf. Small women are not particularly prized in a culture where a woman needs muscle, but I was sure Lois' bounce more than made up for her size. I despaired of getting her to sit still long enough for an interview.

"Lois has ten children," Ludia whispered to me. "I believe seven are still home. Her husband is Solomon Buteng'e. He is away for three weeks out of four, teaching theological education by extension. Lois raises the children—and farms, of course. She also leads the local women's group. The way these women are coming to help her today shows what a well-liked leader she is. She's probably been working since dawn."

Several more guests had now wandered into the house to listen to our interview. The cadre of young wives was outside, boiling water, plucking the chicken, and gathering firewood. Lois herself came in and perched lightly, poised to run.

"You certainly have energy," I laughed.

"No one ever thought I'd live long enough to have a family," she replied. "My twin sister, Esther, and I were scrawny and sickly babies—very small. My mother died four days after we were born. Relatives suggested my father should take us to the mission. They knew that he couldn't take care of us.

"They also knew the tradition: In our tribe one or both twins were usually thrown out into the bush. The smallest one was allowed to die, for sure. Twins were unlucky, a bad omen to the family." [This seemed to be a widespread practice in the old days, in various countries I visited.]

"I was the smallest one. I don't know if the clan would have thrown me away or not. But my father brought us to the mission one Sunday morning. Several missionaries were there. He offered us to them. He wasn't too healthy himself and only wore a piece of cloth knotted over one shoulder.

" 'What! You're not going to accept those rats, are you?' gasped the neighbors when they saw the scrawny babies. But the missionaries accepted us, even though they knew we'd take a lot of care. If they hadn't, we would have died.

"We were put into the hands of Mama Rebecca Mutemwa. She was a widow and the housemother of the Mugongo Girls' School. We were brought up in the dormitory, with the young girls helping. The missionaries took turns sitting up with us at night; we were often very sick with measles and other things. Everyone helped raise us.

"We loved Mama Rebecca and came to see her as our mother. She gave with her whole being. She never had a spirit of tribalism and loved the girls as though there were no differences. So all the girls loved her. She knew lots of things. She knew all the traditional patterns for making baskets and sieves. We liked to watch her work. She helped Esther and me in things of both body and spirit and helped us get good husbands. I praise God for her!

"Esther and I thanked God for Scofu [Bishop] and Mama Wenger and Phoebe Yoder, too. They gave to us with such a pure heart. They nursed us when we were sick. And Mama Wenger had a baby of her own at that time. They saw to it we had uniforms and school fees. They taught us the ways of God. God will have to pay them; we can't! Without them I would not be alive today.

"When I was still a young child, I heard the preaching of revival evangelist Rebecca Makura and felt called by Jesus. I felt that I would put myself on Jesus' side. Jesus would help me every day and give me more of his spirit. Many young girls found new salvation. There was crying, singing, confessing. We were part of the East African revival movement. It was a powerful time."

About the Mugongo Girls' School, Lois' home, another former pupil had said, "We girls were like goats, there were so many of us!"

Miriam, or "Mama," Wenger had started the school to help girls move beyond the narrow, hard confines of their lives. The girls wore white dresses and head scarves and learned to sing beautifully. They were an impressive sight to envious little girls in the village. Studies were kept simple. Basic chores of carrying water and digging fields were included. Christian boys came there to look for Christian wives, in a radical departure from the old ways of arranging marriages. To ease the transition, Bishop Wenger would act as go-between with the parents.

Esther and Lois were identical. The older girls treated them as pets but couldn't always tell them apart. They were lively and appealing little girls.

The twins' father had died, but sometimes their real brothers and sisters would come to visit. "We enjoyed this," Lois remembers, "although there was a language barrier. We were Wakuria, but we were being raised among the Wajita. We managed to make ourselves understood.

"Then when we were twelve or thirteen years old, our brother came and tried to convince us to run away with him, so we could be circumcised and married. The Wakuria used to practice a severe female circumcision. Marriage usually followed soon after. This was the only way to be well regarded as an adult in the tribe. My sister and I, however, knew very little about our own village customs. We were frightened and refused our brother.

"But he didn't give up and tried several times to convince us. The mission was our world. We were very frightened at the idea of leaving it. After that the Wengers arranged for us to visit friends in Nyabange for two weeks, where we would be safer.

"When I was older I knew Solomon Buteng'e because he had come to Mugongo to study. We knew each other a long time. He went to Mama Rebecca and to the missionaries and to my brothers and asked them for me.

"Bishop Wenger had signed a contract with my father the day he brought us to the mission that said we would be married at age eighteen with a bride-price of twelve cows and some goats. One cow was to go to the mission and the others to my brothers, and that is what happened. This was standard for mission-arranged marriages.

"My sister Esther also married and had nine children. She had a very fine family, too. She died in 1979, at age thirty-eight."

Lois had a lively tenor-range laugh and talked a mile a minute. But she became more serious as she said, "I see through my whole life how God has kept me. He gave me a home, a husband, children. He gave me of himself, just as the missionaries did. 'For God so loved the world that he gave his only Son . . .' that is the verse that means the most to me, John 3:16. It reminds me that both God and the missionaries gave of themselves to love me."

Lois' husband was groomed for church leadership and chosen to study at Bukiroba Bible School. After their marriage he was called as a church leader to Ikoma-Robanda and to the Bumange District of Tanzania. Due to his assignments, the family also lived in Nyabange, Nyeraro, Tarime, Mwanza, and Mugumu.

Since his ordination in 1969, Buteng'e has been pastor, district pastor, church treasurer, hospital administrator, and teacher. In all this moving around, Lois has had to leave both good friends and crops behind. She, as farmer and provider of the family food, has had to be flexible, making do with what she could find in each new environment.

"So many times we left when potatoes were in the ground or the sorghum was ripe. We would be ready to harvest and then get called by the church to go! When we moved from Mwanza," she said laughing, "the chairs and the beds broke. The chickens died. Aiiee!

"My husband continues to be called by God. His teaching work means he is gone several weeks out of every month. I'm happy because we are doing God's work. But sometimes I get upset and resist. Then I have nothing. It's only when I feel it is God's work that my life has meaning."

Lois leaned forward in her typically energetic style, as though to physically catch the thought she was looking for. "Sometimes I feel sorry for myself, and I think, *I'm left here in Mugumu with the children and all the work*. When that happens, I pray that I will be able to accept the work God has given me to do, both housework and church work. I pray that he will give me the strength to do it."

Lois certainly seems to have been given the strength. She loves to sing and is famous for the joycries she raises in church. She hosts many guests in her home, runs a self-sufficient homestead, raises her children, and sponsors the local women's group. When there are church conferences, she makes arrangements for food and gets volunteers to help prepare it.

"I want our women's group to go ahead in spirit. It is hard to be a leader, because each person has her own problems. We know what needs there are in development, but not what needs there are in the heart.

"These days we are all planting, so we don't meet so much. But we learn sewing, knitting, and handiwork together. We made our own dresses from sewing bundles the North Americans sent us."

Lois' life is spent doing vigorous, tangible work. For fun she sings and laughs with friends. She is not given to abstract philosophy. But she is able to focus clearly on what is important.

"I'd just like to keep loving God more," Lois said, her eyes sparkling. "If I'd go away from God, I'd forget where I came from, where I've been."

Now in middle age, Lois has a rich life. She has ten fine children and five grandchildren, two of whom are twins—precious twins to constantly remind her of where she came from and where she is going.

5. Janet—Straddling Two Cultures

Janet Mmanywa. Born 1944, Mnyamwezi tribe, Sikonge village, Tabora region, Tanzania.

I first visited Janet Mmanywa in her row-house home in Bethlehem, Pennsylvania. There she would run up and down the stairs ten times a day, so she would not get soft living in America.

I liked her immediately. She was my own age, with only a secondary school education. Yet she had already managed to sit astride several cultures at once and to do it gracefully. She spoke three languages fluently, was a well-respected church leader among women at home in Tanzania, and preached with confidence and charisma in American pulpits. She was comfortable in Tanzanian villages as well as the American city. Her eyes were quiet and calm, but full of purpose. Her one goal while here in the States was to learn useful things to take home to help women and young girls there.

Edward, her retired-dentist husband, was finishing at Moravian Seminary that year. Her son, Lucas, was just beginning his first year at the college. Three daughters were adjusting well to American public schools. African guests were always running in and out of their house, friends from the local Moravian church dropped in to offer to run errands, and the phone kept ringing. *Welcome to America,* I kept thinking with a grin. The family had been sent to the United States for study to prepare for leadership in the Tanzanian church.

"I am looking for an outlet for good quality fabric dyes," Janet told me. "In Tanzania we try to teach the women projects which will help them earn some money. We have tried to teach the art of batik. But then we cannot get the dyes from outside the country because our currency has been devalued. We have tried natural dyes, but they are mostly yellow and brown, not the favorite colors, and they don't last as well."

Another time she said, "I am looking for a class which teaches how to make one's own sewing patterns. That is something the women would love to learn back home.

"Cake decorating is something city women could do as a

small business. Where can I learn that?" Janet's whole focus was on the ministry waiting for her back home.

She spoke eloquently at our commissioning service, telling her personal testimony. A sturdy, short woman with a pleasant alto voice, she became beautiful as she preached, exuding a charisma and a glow which moved our congregation.

Janet's father had been a teacher in Moravian schools. The oldest child and very bright, Janet was his favorite. He loved explaining things to her. She remembers drifting off to sleep at night while her father was still talking to her. He was a firmly Western-oriented man. The church had enveloped the family in its ceremonies of baptism and communion.

But one day Ugandans came preaching Jesus Christ as their Savior. "It took some time for the people to understand this," Janet remembered. "But my father was born again. I remember. I saw changes in our family life. I learned then that Christianity was an inner and not just a cultural change.

"We moved around as my father accepted various teaching jobs. The moves usually meant my parents had to learn a new tribal language and new customs. But travel made us all see things in different ways.

"At eighteen I graduated from Bwiru Secondary School at Mwanza and became a social worker. My husband's parents met me there and suggested me as a wife for their son. He then approached my parents. I felt myself too young for marriage and would have enjoyed secretarial school, but my parents insisted on the marriage. In those days, parents were afraid for their daughters. They feared bad things would happen to them, and they would get pregnant. So they thought a good marriage prospect was a blessing."

Edward Mmanywa was a handsome, intelligent young man who would become a dentist and a leader. In spite of this, Janet's difficult years now began. She had two babies within two years, and her marriage was not stable.

She felt unloved and full of tears as she boarded a train for a slow two-day trip back to her parents' home. She brought her toddler, Rhoda, and Lucas, a baby who struggled with a hiatal hernia and threw up his food constantly. There was no money for an operation.

"I called Edward 'that man' then," Janet said laughing, "and I announced bitterly to my parents that I was not going back to that man!

"My father asked his whole congregation to pray. 'I believe God can change your husband,' he kept insisting. I didn't believe it. I wasn't interested in forgiveness or reconciliation.

"Two months later, I received my first letter from Edward. 'Come home,' he wrote, 'I've come to the Lord.'

"I was wary, but my father was ecstatic, convinced this was the answer to the prayers of his church. 'You must go,' he insisted over my protests. 'My door is open if it doesn't work out.' So I had no choice. I left for Dar es Salaam grudgingly.

"When I arrived, Edward met me at the station. When I saw him, I knew the change was for real. His face was different.

"I observed my husband and saw that positive attitudes were replacing old habits. Now that I could no longer blame someone else, my own sin became apparent. At last I found that though I was a Christian, I needed Jesus Christ to change my heart, too."

From that time on the couple had a mutual basis, their faith in Christ, from which to work. Even so, Janet said, "Marriage must be worked at. It is difficult, even for Christians. It takes patience from both people.

"I would tell myself, 'Just put water in your mouth!' (I meant, don't allow yourself to talk back. Think it over). And we have a good saying: Being patient doesn't kill.

"I hope my daughters will have enough education to earn their own money after marriage. To be able to pay for the things her heart desires makes a woman feel like herself, free. What you need for your heart comes from yourself. This makes for much less quarreling in a marriage.

"In our culture, the man controls his money, and the woman, if she doesn't have her own money, must ask for everything. This causes pain in the heart to ask and even worse pain when one is refused.

"I decided for myself, after we were born again, to talk this over with my husband. I decided to raise poultry. I began with fifty chickens and got my flock up to five hundred. We ran the household on my money and banked Edward's income. I felt good. I felt free! Edward would joke, 'I must give her parents more dowry for her.'"

Janet had four young children within five years, raised her poultry, and kept an "open house."

"I sometimes had fifteen to twenty relatives or needy people in our house. I always was giving away my own clothes to others who needed them."

On top of all this work, each child's birth had been hard and dangerous. Janet was prone to hemorrhage. Finally she quietly sought out birth control information. When several years went by with no more babies, Janet's mother chided her. The culture encouraged bearing as many children as possible. The Bible told them to be fruitful. Sensitive to the social pressure, Janet bore two more children. Edward made sure her blood was taken ahead of time for transfusions.

Janet herself encouraged family planning. She admitted, "Our culture is in confusion. We are in the process of deciding for ourselves which traditions are healthy and which ones to drop. The missionaries, for example, taught us never to plait our hair or wear jewelry. And our pastors forbade us to dance at weddings. But now we younger Christians are trying to put our faith into our own cultural setting. We love to dance all night at weddings. The bride sits and listens and the older women sing advice songs about marriage.

"It's important for us to be clear with the older church members so they understand our decisions. Edward and I will ask a dowry for our girls. The money is a gift to the mother and to the relatives. We feel it is a good custom.

"But there are others we want to change. Grandparents, for example, are supposed to teach their grandchildren about sex. Many times a child will ask a question, and we say, 'Am I your grandmother? Ask her.' Thus the young people do not have enough information. Many young girls are pregnant before marriage. We need to be more open, teach more.

"I am so concerned about women and young girls, especially those not able to continue school. Young girls are idle, have no challenge, no opportunities for further training.

"I try to encourage mothers to stop being so busy, to take time to listen and talk with their children. Women have to work so hard it is easy to give away the relationship. I'm constantly looking for ideas to teach to women's groups to help them earn some money."

After Edward Mmanywa had been a dentist for twenty years and he and Janet had long been active in the church, the local Moravian bishop called Edward in to his sickroom. Later he invited Janet in for her solitary talk. "You should work for the church," he told her.

"I saw it as an individual call," Janet said soberly. He called my husband as well, but he was also saying it to me. Edward and I were like his children."

The church wrote to the Tanzanian president Nyerere himself, requesting that Edward be released from his government position as dentist. Surprisingly, the government agreed and even granted a modest pension. Edward could now train for the ministry. Janet's only sorrow was that the old bishop did not live long enough to see this.

In Janet's new role, she has tried to be advocate for women. For example, the national church disciplines pregnant unmarried young women by excommunicating them for six months to one year. Nothing is done to the man.

Janet thinks many policies need reevaluation. "Many of our church policies were formed during the last generation. Our pastors here have conflicting views. We are in a difficult time of change. In Tanzania we have only one church, the Christian Church of Tanzania. All denominations must give up their differences and agree together on rules and doctrine so that we can be *one* in the eyes of the Muslims and African traditionalists. If we can cooperate and show them we are one, it is a powerful witness."

While in Africa, I received a depressed letter from Janet.

"Pray for me," she wrote. "I am so depressed. You see, I am pregnant. We did not plan for this to happen. It is not only dangerous for me at my age, but we have no medical insurance for this. American fees are so high! We have already asked the Moravian Church for extra help in various instances and feel we cannot ask them again.

"I just want to quietly sneak home to Africa and give up. It is humiliating. You know how Americans are. They say, 'How did it happen?' How can an African woman answer that? We don't talk about such things. But the Americans are closed in about their feelings, so I feel I cannot speak about my true feelings of homesickness and despair."

Janet went through a true winter of despair in 1986. Later she told me, "Of course, my problem was pride. I wanted to learn things, be a leader, take a course or two.

"When I could finally put my pride down, there was all sorts of love and support available. Women came to visit and brought everything I needed for the baby. The church board agreed to pay our medical expenses. Edward helped all he could. I had a good doctor who controlled my hemorrhaging. When I could accept it with humility, there was love all around me. God was there in that experience, teaching me something about trusting him."

Janet's seventh child is named Hope, an extraordinarily beautiful and robust baby. Hope was all Janet had to cling to that winter, she says. Now she has a new strength, a new assurance of God's presence with her in her weakness. She loves her new daughter deeply.

When I got home and visited Janet, their belongings were strewn in open suitcases as they packed to leave. Hope was the charming center of the family activity. Edward had already returned to Tanzania. Janet would close up the house and travel alone with the children.

The family was asked to return to a rural church in an undeveloped area. Janet was firmly committed to this. She wanted to show that, despite their education, their first priority was the poor and meek of this world. There would be no electricity or other Western amenities.

But she knew that the children would be able to adjust. "Eventually it is probable that we'll be called to work in church administration," she said. "But we want to give this rural church a boost first.

"My desire is to share the love of God, which I have seen and discovered for myself. I want to help in little ways where I can."

CHAPTER

The Childless

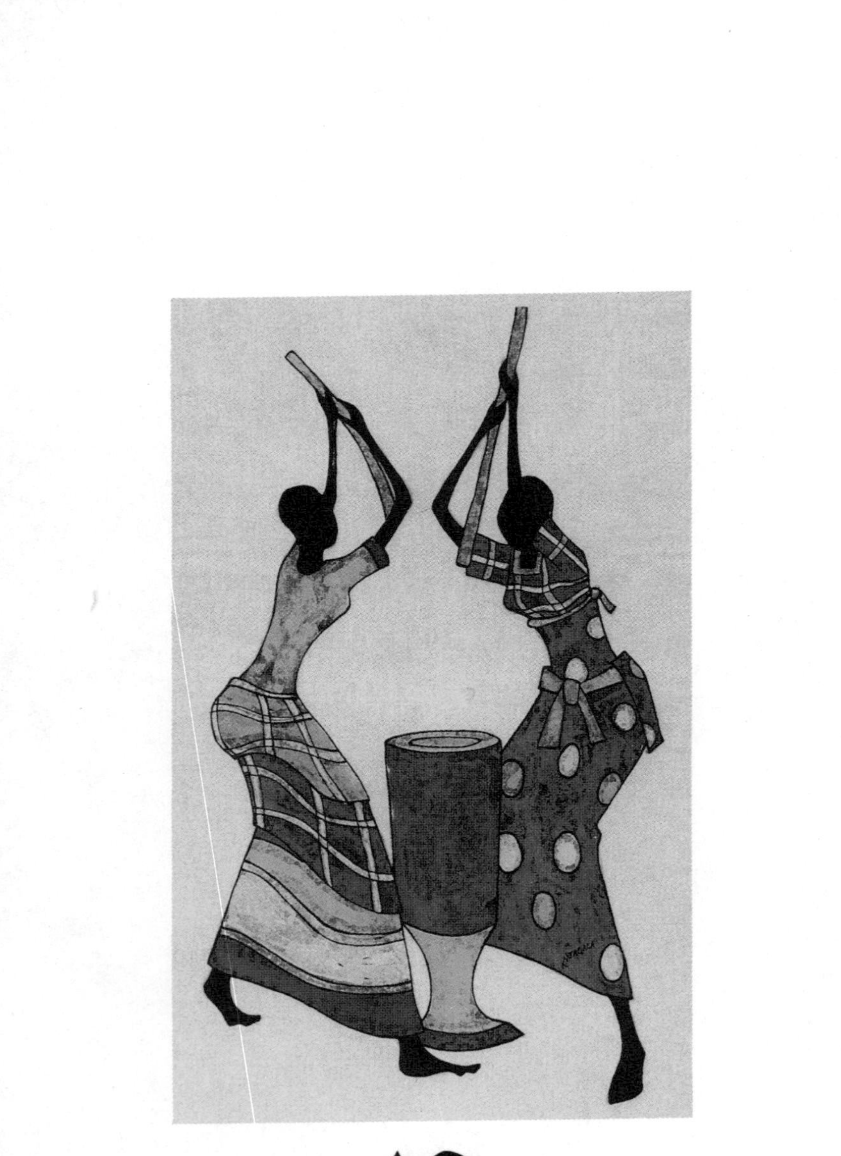

1. Shirati, Tanzania

Tanzania, the former Tanganyika and the island of Zanzibar now combined into one nation, reminded most of us of public television specials. We thought of the great Serengeti plain, the Ngorongoro Crater, the snow-capped Mount Kilimanjaro, and perhaps Leakey's famous archaeological digs in Olduvai Gorge. There is a large country, however, south of these tourist attractions. It reaches six hundred miles from the Indian Ocean to Lake Victoria, and eight hundred miles from Kilimanjaro south to the dangerous border of Mozambique.

In the interior, busy villages go about their business in old-fashioned, time-honored ways, often without electricity or piped water.

Tanzania has charm. The rural people are gracious. They love music and laughter. They revere their gentleman statesman, Julius Nyerere, who led the country from its independence to his voluntary semi-retirement in 1987. A true Christian at heart, Nyerere is one of the few African leaders who did not gain great personal wealth at the expense of his country. In fact, as an example to them, he now teaches school part-time near his country home.

Unfortunately, Nyerere's economic policies were idealistic rather than helpful. Tanzania's economy was bankrupt. In 1967, when socialism was formally instituted, land, banks, businesses, and institutions were nationalized. Even the church came under some government control. People and isolated villages were relocated. They were moved to larger villages where farming was centrally organized and schools were available. Indian businesses were now government owned and run. Their owners were evicted. Unfortunately, systems broke down and stopped working.

Today, Tanzania's currency is worthless on foreign exchanges. This means that when Western-made factory parts break down, they must be imported with scarce Western currency, not shillings. Most things stay broken.

This causes strange situations. In Bukiroba, women grow cotton for the local mill, which weaves it into cloth and dyes colorful, local patterns onto it. Despite its popularity, the cloth is unavailable locally, even to tourists. This is because the factory owners must sell it for foreign currency, not shillings, to keep operating. The cloth is all exported.

People live on the land. Most have low incomes. The highest paid church officers make about thirty-eight dollars per month. A good rooster, meanwhile, costs about six dollars. Obviously people are unable to buy much, even when goods are available. And whether goods are available or not is always a gamble. There are periodic shortages of sugar, flour, rice, fuel oil, and petrol.

Tanzanians do not complain however. Village people may have reverted to old ways of doing things, but they are consoled by a widespread pride. Tanzania did not experience a period of violence after independence. It did not rely on Western money or leaders. It is an independent nation with its own homegrown socialistic system. If it has not brought the people wealth, it is still their own experiment. They will own the consequences. Tanzanians like themselves.

The Tanzania I loved best was not the busy coastal capital, Dar es Salaam, with its Moslem population or even the expensive game park lodges with their English meals. It was the village life in the west, along Lake Victoria. There people speak both Kiswahili and their own tribal language, but rarely English. They are friendly and hospitable toward guests and feed them generously, knowing that guests always bring blessing to a house. Life is simple here, but full of local intrigue, gossip, the high drama of human life lived at close quarters with others.

I sat on the porch of the tiny guest house and rested, enjoying the village sounds. It was a long way from Nairobi. No traffic blaring. No crowds. Here I smelled the sun on dry grass and the little goats. The roads were only deep ruts over bare ground. The lake water had to be carefully strained and boiled.

Behind our house a woman pounded cassava with her mortar and pestle with a rhythmic, hollow "thlunk—thlunk." The same beat woke me that morning at sunrise. The large boulders strewn here and there were covered with chipped white cassava, sweating a sour-milk smell as it dried in the sun.

Cassava, or manioc, is a staple food in areas where rainfall is uncertain. It is not particularly nutritious, but has the virtue of growing in drought and infertile, sandy soil. The large roots can stay in the ground without rotting until they are needed. Women farmers dig up the starchy roots and soak them for several days to remove the cyanide in them.

During this soak the cassava begins to ferment, adding a slightly sour flavor good cooks prize. Then the roots are chipped into small pieces and spread to dry in the sun.

When dry the cassava is pounded or ground into flour and stirred into boiling water to produce a porridge which is a bit like mashed potatoes. This has a variety of names— *ugali, foufou,* or *sadzha*. It is eaten all over East Africa by rolling bits into a ball and dipping it into meat, fish, or vegetable sauce. For most Africans, if you have not had some cassava or maize porridge that day, you have not eaten.

Chris has learned with delight that every time he stepped out of our quarters with his battered soccer ball, an instant swarm of boys would show up, ready to play. Many of them were quite good. They practiced on homemade balls made from rags. I hurt for the younger boys who sat on the sidelines, uninvited by their older brothers, envy showing in their eyes, arms hugging their bare legs. The laughter in the bright, clear air reminded me of children's playgrounds everywhere.

The boys came from the small leper colony below our house.

My stomach lurched at first when I heard that term—leper colony. But it was just another village. Shirati is a town built around a thriving church-run hospital.

Part of its early reputation came from its good leprosy work. The middle-aged and older people who had leprosy in the old days are no longer infectious but need to be monitored. Many still live with the grim remnants of the disease. Unfortunately, numb extremities do not rejuvenate. They still get burned, infected, and cause endless trouble. Crude orthopedic devices are available at Shirati, unlike other areas where we saw cripples pulling themselves along in the thick dust, on their stomachs.

Many early leper patients were sent to Shirati by their horrified families and then forgotten. Eventually they formed new marriages and alliances with each other and came to see this village as home. They remained there, eking out small subsistence farms like everyone else, living under the hospital's reassuring care. They formed their own church. Seeing their children, those big healthy boys, I smiled. Love could hardly produce more tangible results.

Lisen and Bob improvised a rope washline to hang our laundry on. Someone had to guard our clothes while they dried. But at least in this climate that took only an hour or so, even though they were washed and wrung out by hand and were heavy with water.

Someone had tethered a goat to a bush in our yard, evidently called somewhere else in a hurry. I volunteered to watch while I wrote, and I sat on the porch enjoying the cooling breeze from Lake Victoria, only two miles away. Random thoughts of our life in Shirati coursed through my mind.

One day the weekly women's prayer group brought their tools, and instead of praying, we hoed. Prayer of a different kind. Some sixty women attacked a small plot next to the church with laughter, conversation, and teasing. Nurses from the hospital, though barefoot, worked in their stiff, white uniforms. Others wrapped old kangas around pretty, polyester dresses. To save our shoes, most of us took them off and enjoyed the cool, freshly-turned, red earth between our toes.

The heavy hoe was swung like a pickax. The weight of the

broad head lifted the dry earth in clods. It was hard work, woman's work. The ground wasn't raked fine, but left in clumps to better absorb the torrential tropical rains when they came in a week or two.

The old women got the light work; they followed us and planted peanuts (groundnuts). This cash crop would yield the women money for their treasury, money to provide small sums for those who were sick or hungry. The old women bent double at the waist to plant, knees straight, making bright red and yellow triangles as they moved through the field.

I borrowed my hoe from a fifty-year-old leprosy victim, hoping to let her rest a bit. Her fingers were disfigured, and she limped badly. I took a spot next to an eight-months-pregnant young woman, set my jaw, and promised myself not to rest until she did.

She set a slow pace but never stopped. In true Western style, my pace was quick. Start and stop, rest and run.

In an hour the field had been prepared and planted. "Let the rains come!" Women drifted away, talking louder over their shoulders as they walked, still not saying good-bye. Some headed for the daily 5:00 p.m. choir practice at the church. Others moved to gather their children and prepare for the hot meal of ugali, greens, and sauce, served after dark.

Again I focused on the adolescent boys before me, their strong, brown legs flashing over the soccer ball. Their sisters were at home, working. It is the women who feed the families, a task that must probe some deep primal instincts in women everywhere.

I thought of the cozy cooking fires after dark, with children gathered around, and thought of women the world over, cooking, tirelessly protecting their young, offering special tidbits to husband and guests. I thought of co-wives, taking turns at carrying a husband's food to him, tempting him to come to her quarters that night. In East Africa men are supposed to provide protection and meat for the pot. Women provide the fire, fuel, water, and clean clothes; they cook, farm, process food, and produce children. And like women anywhere, they use food to show love, hospitality to others, enjoying the giving of the gift.

In the old days, there were many customs and taboos surrounding the eating of food. Now these seem to be disappearing. Many tribes had a taboo against women eating eggs or chicken, delicacies reserved for men. There were varied rules for pregnant, menstruating, or lactating women.

Often the women and children ate last, waiting endlessly until the man of the family came home, so he could eat first. In some tribes women served the food to their husbands on their knees, eyes cast down, without speaking. Even today, except among young couples, there is still this segregation, women serving men and eating later whatever is left.

For centuries these rules must have ensured that the warriors were kept strong, for without them the whole tribe could have been decimated. Today the rules no longer work. Over half the village women are chronically anemic, denied their fair share of scarce protein, even during their frequent pregnancies.

There were other taboos, however, designed to protect women. In many tribes couples were counseled against having intercourse while a woman was pregnant, lactating or menstruating, and after her menopause. There is still an undercurrent of puritanical belief that intercourse is, for the woman, only for the creation of life. She is not expected to enjoy it. All that abstinence gave the woman a longer span between pregnancies. It also favored polygamy as husbands looked for another woman to fill in the long gaps.

There is usually a good reason for everything, even though I can't understand it, I reminded myself for the thousandth time.

My mind veered to a conversation a month earlier. I was flying to Zaire alone, sandwiched between two United Nations officials. The Englishman on my left declared, with evangelical enthusiasm, "My commission studies pure water availability. That is Africa's primary need—clean running water. It will revolutionize people's lives. When women are no longer tied to back-breaking labor and their children get healthier, modernization is inevitable."

An hour later, the Swiss fellow on my right identified himself as a lawyer on a United Nations commission dedicated to teaching international law. He said, "Once Africans learn their legal rights in import and export, their economies will flourish. They will enter the world community as equals, not debtors. This will revolutionize their countries."

I had reservations about these two men, with their advice and their big budgets. But I was delighted to have found a lawyer. "Could you help me understand?" I asked. "I have been speaking to women. It seems to me that tribal laws are often punitive against women and children. Are there modern laws to protect them?"

"Oh yes," he said. "Women have equal rights under many of the new African constitutions. They just don't know it yet. Many people are afraid to push against old customs for fear that some relative, alive or recently dead, will practice witchcraft against them."

"You must remember," the lawyer said, "that social mores and customs changed very slowly in ancient times. They kept a culture stable. Their effectiveness was proved by how well the culture survived. You may not understand the customs or what they were meant to preserve. But you need to see that they worked. They always worked. If they didn't, they would have been dropped as the tribe decreased in power.

"Sometimes the goals of ancient customs were much different from our own, so we don't understand them. Sometimes, for example, a culture is willing to sacrifice individual rights for the good of the group. In Africa the survival of the group has been paramount. Try looking at customs from that perspective."

On the porch at Shirati, waiting for the wash to dry, I remembered that advice. I opened my notebook of jottings from many places. Perhaps I would have time to think about specific customs which had upset me; I would try to look at them from the perspective of group survival. I read through pages of notes. My eyes noted these excerpts:

- In Africa, the social units are family, village, clan, tribe, nation, in decreasing importance. Clan loyalty is very strong, and membership is often recognized by names. Clan leaders are consulted for marriages, funerals, judgments in disputes. Each person feels tremendous social pressure to be well thought of in the clan community.
- In the old days, and still today in village areas, individuals did not own land. The clan had territorial rights over certain areas and assigned farm plots to families. A man was expected to build a shelter and view this area as his homestead. Even if he lived and worked in the city, this was home for the man. He was to help care for his parents, take responsibilities in his clan, bring in a wife to build a family, and be buried there.
- From birth on, females were expected to leave. A girl would marry when she was only twelve to sixteen years old. She would go away to her husband's place and remain there except for visits home. She and her children would help the husband's clan, not her own, grow stronger. There was no expectation that the woman would help her parents in their old age, although she sometimes did. Rather, she was expected to be responsible to and for her parents-in-law. She was expected to be adaptable, to adopt her husband's faith and customs. She had to obey his parents, and fit in. In many tribes, the children belonged to and stayed with the father in case of divorce.
- If a woman chose to leave the marriage or was "chased away" (their term), her family was obligated to return all or at least some of the bride-price. This was usually next to impossible. There was a strong societal pressure on her to do her best, remain in her new place, and work hard.
- Because the woman was mobile, usually leaving her own clan to be married, she often owned no property. All property, owned by the males of the clans, thus stayed within the clan forever. She did not inherit from her husband or father.
- A woman's brother often benefited most from her bride-price because it gave the family wealth to begin negotiations for the son's bride. At the same time, he was then expected to be

his sister's lifelong protector. If she was ill-treated, he was supposed to exert pressure on her husband. If she returned home, it was the brothers who had to support her. Uncles were expected to help their sisters' children along and often contributed to school fees and small expenses. In these years of transition, however, brothers may be reluctant to fill these roles.

- The family usually demanded a bride-price to compensate for the loss of the daughter and her offspring. In prosperous times, the bride-price was high enough that a young man had to ask for help from his family and clan to get together the herd of goats and cows, the palm wine, or money needed. Payment came back to the parents, uncles, brothers, and others to whom favors were owed. In this way, two entire clans were involved in complicated financial dealings and obligations over this marriage. This encouraged both sides to keep their promises and maintain the marriage well.

There had been intricate balances, all designed to keep the clans growing and interdependent, I thought to myself. Like European royalty matches, there was purpose in all this financial finagling and the intermarriages between clans within the tribe. But, yes, women took the brunt of it.

Women were the courageous ones. They left their families in early adolescence, with no belongings except their clothes. Their only wealth was a fertile womb by which they could earn status and eternal ties to the living and the dead.

It was no wonder, I thought, that young girls began childbearing early and with such determination. Their children would bring them security, wealth, place, and would remember them after they die. It was sons, not husbands, who would love and respect them and provide for them when they were old.

But the system breaks down for the woman who cannot conceive. Childlessness is a major theme in Africa, as it was in the Old Testament. The barren girl is a pariah. Her husband regards her as a false promise, a dead end. She is a shriveled vine that will produce nothing to connect her to the afterlife.

There are not many accurate statistics about the frequency of infertility in developing countries. With overpopulation a major problem, most governments are not interested in underwriting studies or research on infertility. However, it is apparent that infertility is higher than in North America, for example. For one thing, only the most basic medical procedures are available to women seeking help to conceive. Even these are usually outside the financial scope of most families since they usually are available only at private hospitals.

Venereal disease is epidemic and untreated in large areas of Africa where good medical care is not available. Chronic uterine and bladder infections are common in women among those who practice the more severe types of circumcision. These are obviously factors contributing to infertility among African women. The Maasai tribe of Kenya, for instance, has an abnormally high rate of infertility, and both of the above factors contribute.

Some tribes traditionally alleviate some of the pressure by making sure a girl is pregnant before the marriage was considered to be complete. Others value virginity before the ceremonies. But neither boys nor girls are considered adults or valued members of the clan until they marry and have several children.

Some childless women are sent back to their families. If the husband is this callous, he will probably ask for at least some of the bride-price back. This further humiliates the woman, who knows how hard this will be for her family.

Others must make room for a second wife and help her raise her children. She then theoretically becomes boss of the new wife. However, if the new wife has children, she may flaunt her favored position, creating an intolerable situation as well as lowered status for the first wife.

For Christian men, a wife's infertility is agonizing. Some men hold out until their Christian wives reach menopause before marrying a young wife. But they are rare. African men often marry more wives, not out of lust, but out of a deep desire for progeny, the more the better. African men who have fathered no children are scarcely respected and have no sense of being part of an eternal flow of life into eternity. They are literally cut off.

Infertile men are protected by custom, in that many tribes encourage the wives to get pregnant with someone else, preferably a brother-in-law. The children belong to the husband, and his honor is still intact.

A childless woman, on the other hand, retains little respect. "Prostitutes. Women who live alone in the city without husband or children are usually prostitutes," the other women told me. "How else could they get by?"

I met a surprising amount of suspicion and hostility from both sexes against any woman who lived alone. When a man chases away a woman who cannot produce children, none of her choices are pleasant.

Yes, I was forced to admit it. The tribal systems had worked toward the survival of the group. Even today rugged individualism scarcely exists in East Africa. But when sacrifices had to be made, it was usually women who were to make them. Faces of some of these women came to me as I rested in Shirati—strong, beautiful, pain-wracked faces.

In a village on the edge of Kenya, I met a traditional woman of sixty-one who looked as if she had been born in another century. She was ill, unkempt, hungry, and wore a perpetual scowl to hide her fear. Rioba was doll-sized, about four feet, ten inches tall, with a shaved head and stretched earlobes. She seemed very old. Perhaps it was her diet, mostly cassava, which gave her dizzy spells and headaches when she carried her firewood and water. She lived in a rented thatched cottage and lived on the few pennies she could earn selling vegetables in a tiny, village market. She had not a relative left in the world.

As a young girl, Rioba married a man she liked. She felt happy about the marriage. Over the next fourteen years, six children were born to her. Each one, at the age of four or five, died after a one- or two-day illness. Finally her husband chased her away, followed her back to her parents' house and retrieved his bride-price. This he used to marry another woman. Many people believed that a woman like Rioba carried a cloud of misfortune with her and that a future with her would be hopeless.

Rioba lived for fifteen years on the compound with her brothers. Then the last one died. The past fifteen years she had spent alone, frightened, lonely, too tired to stay clean or well-fed.

When I impulsively gave her a gift of a red-checkered blouse from my suitcase, her scowl dissolved. She hugged me in her tiny arms, her little bare-skinned head resting on my shoulder. She murmured over and over, "Mtoto wangu, mtoto wangu!" (My child, my child).

I also met a lovely young woman named Perusi, dressed well in a kanga and pretty head scarf. She met Jan Shetler and me on the path as she returned home from her office job in the district church headquarters of Bukiroba, Tanzania.

"You must come home with me so I can make you some tea," she laughingly insisted. We yielded to her pleading and headed for a neat, tin-roofed home some distance away.

Perusi had had a lot of promise. She married a handsome, young Christian, and the two churchworkers were full of hope for the future. They had charm and intelligence. Both hoped to make a real contribution to the church and community.

One fatal flaw had developed. Perusi did not get pregnant. They waited and prayed. Perusi's friends and relatives prayed. The church prayed. Nothing.

Finally, her young husband bowed to the inevitable. Not having any children was for him unthinkable. His family recommended a girl and brought her to him.

Now Perusi busied herself making us lemon grass tea in the backyard. Jan Shetler, the local development worker, and I sat on straight chairs and chatted with her husband and his second wife. He had a good job in a bank and liked his work. He had been forced to withdraw from the church, however, and he now practiced the spiritual part of his life in solitude. The house was tiny but housed them all.

I watched Perusi's husband swoop the smallest child into his lap and grin at her affectionately. The house was filled with children's laughter and a mother's scolding. The children would grow up calling both women "mother."

But for Perusi, behind her gay smile, there would be perpetual pain. In the eyes of others, there would always be something missing in her. And when she saw that tenderness on her husband's face as he fondled his children, she would feel only despair. Yet I knew Perusi would not give up.

The childless women who created lives for themselves in a "dry desert land," happy confident women, these are the ones I love to remember: irrepressible Perusi; tall, dignified Mariamu; homely, round Priscila; grandmotherly, old Prisca, with one eyeball rolling as she sat in the sun. Each had found a place, a niche, as a child of God, that transcended circumstance. These were the women I would never forget.

2. Priscila—And Her Elderly Husband

Priscila Aumba. Born 1934, Luo tribe, Awendo, Kenya. Shirati, Tanzania.

We followed a footpath that veered off the main market street of Shirati. It headed away from the mission hospital and out toward Oboke, the rock-scarred hill overlooking the town. *All that open space out there,* I marveled, *yet these houses are almost on top of each other.*

Many looked just alike. The burned bricks were a pale mud color, and a tin roof kept out the rain. Most had wooden shutters for windows. There were no obvious water facilities other than Lake Victoria a mile away, shimmering in the distance. Banana plants and papaya trees crowded the yards along with outdoor kitchens and cooking fires. The gardens were usually planted farther out of town.

With not much to distinguish the homes one from the other, I was glad that Loyce, a hometown girl, was along. But at every other house relatives stopped her for a friendly exchange in Swahili. It was already five in the afternoon and the tropical sun dropped promptly at 6:15.

"Who is this Priscila? What is her story?" Loyce asked me again, puzzled. She lived in Dar es Salaam now and was trying to catch up on village life.

"I don't know," I admitted. "Several leaders of the women's group assured me that if I wanted to meet a real Christian, I should talk to Priscila." I shifted my cameras, tape recorder, and notebook to the other sweating shoulder.

"This is it—if my aunt gave me the right directions," Loyce announced. We were in front of a pleasant, mud-brick home with an immaculate peanut garden growing on every available inch surrounding it.

Priscila was in back, building up a cooking fire and starting her supper on a two-hour simmer. She had just come home from her job as a cleaner at the mission hospital. She welcomed us warmly, took us into the house, then moved heavily back to her fire.

Then she chased four boys away from the little sitting room so she could 'talk freely.' The boys went to work on the back steps, flicking off the heads of tiny sardine-like dried fish which would be the base of a fish sauce for their ughali. Several sleek ducks ate the tiny fish heads as the boys worked, often catching them in the air.

Priscila had a kind, weathered, round face. Something about her gait made her seem older than her years. Yet for all her humble, quiet manner, her carriage was confident.

She had obviously gathered her thoughts over the fire. When she joined us, Priscila was ready to begin.

"My parents were not Christians and did not send us to school. When I was fifteen years old, a friend of the family came and asked for me. In a case like that, parents can't very well say no, so I became the second wife of Otieno.

"A year later I began attending the Mennonite church. There I first learned to read. As I came to know what was in the Bible, I repented of my sins and entered into a relationship with Jesus.

"I had no problems in my marriage, but I became convinced that I couldn't be a second wife. My husband already had a wife, and the situation just wasn't right. I decided to leave him. After discussion, the church agreed it would be better that way.

"The following year I married Philemon Ageke, a man as old as my father. I was eighteen years old.

"For four years there was love between us. My husband worked as a watchman at Shirati Hospital. But gradually my husband's thinking grew unclear. He also became impotent.

"If I talked with fellow Christians, he became jealous. He thought I liked that fellowship more than staying home with him. Then things got even worse. If people came to my home for a church meeting, he thought they came to advise me to kill him.

"That thought got stuck in his mind. He was afraid of death and brooded on his suspicions. He was no longer able to work, and I supported us with my job as a cleaner at the hospital. I cleaned all day. Then I came home, dug in my garden and raised our food, cooked, and washed. I worked very hard."

Priscila sighed and sat back in her chair. I thought her husband's symptoms sounded like Alzheimer's disease. I wondered what it had been like, being a young woman in her twenties caring for a senile husband.

"Ageke beat me once. But he was not that type of man, really. Another time he threatened me with a machete, but I stood up to him. When he tried to chase me away, I told him, 'I'm a Christian. I'm not going to break my vow to be your wife. I belong here.'

"Each time, God helped me to cool down and stay.

"Ageke went to the church to ask for their help against me. Then he went repeatedly to the court to accuse me. This is what happened:

> "Does she feed you?"
> "Yes!"
> "Does she clothe you?"
> "Yes."
> "Then what's your problem, old man?"
> "She wants to kill me!"

"Well, the court kept sending him home. When neither the church nor court would do anything, he gradually calmed down.

"I was still a young woman. I thought a lot. I couldn't fulfill my body's desires. I had never borne children. Should I run around and try to get pregnant with someone else? Luo custom would have condoned that. Everyone knows how important it is for a Luo to have lots of children!

"I prayed so much and read my Bible so much to avoid being angry with my husband. And it really did help.

"I thought, *I can't go back and do what I did before I was a Christian. My body is a temple. Rather than desecrate my temple, I will choose not to have children. I will remain in Christ. What I give up in this world, I will have in heaven.*

"I became aware that the boys on the steps had grown silent. They were eavesdropping, shocked like teenagers everywhere to discover that the old were once young and wrestled with dreams and desires.

"One time my husband did chase me away," she sighed, "and I took a room for about three months. I let him live in the house, although I was building it with the money I had saved from my work at the hospital. I could see he was getting wilder and roaming about. I would buy his food and bring it. But no one cooked for him or washed his clothes. Finally I offered to come back and help him because he was suffering. Then I stayed until he died in 1982.

"Surprisingly, before he died he came to love Jesus. He talked about Jesus and prayed in the hours before his death. I was with him. I don't think he could have come to Jesus if I hadn't stayed with him.

"While he was still living I realized I needed to plan for my future. In our tradition it is the sons who support us when we get old. But I had no sons. I saved money from my work at the hospital where I earn about twenty dollars per month. First I bought some roofing, then the burned bricks. I began to build a house.

"I helped raise my husband's little niece after her father died. She married a builder. Her husband came and helped me build my house. Church members helped me set the rafters. It is a good house. Later I saved enough to add a little shed in the back where people can rent a room from me.

"I can't work as hard any more. Sometimes I feel afraid because I am no longer strong. I have pain in my kidneys and in my feet. I still work at the hospital, but I don't dig in my fields as much now.

"Nevertheless, I am praising God! I look back over my life, and I think how I have given up a marriage, my body desires, and having my own children. But God has given me such joy.

"I am at peace in my old age. I have my own house and can make my own way. A special joy is that God has given me a family, after all. My sister and her two young boys live with me. She runs a little restaurant and hires two teenage boys to help her. They live with us too. We all help each other a great deal. This family gives me joy.

"My Christian friends have prayed with me and counseled me over the years. This has strengthened me. I served on the church council for a few years, and I am active in the women's *chama*, or organization. So I have close Christian friends."

Priscila opened her worn Luo Bible and together we read Isaiah 55:3, she in Luo and I in English:

> Ho, every one who thirsts, come to the waters; and he who has no money, come, buy and eat! Come, buy wine and milk without money and without price. Why do you spend your money for that which is not bread, and your labor for that which does not satisfy? Hearken diligently to me, and eat what is good, and delight yourselves in fatness. Incline your ear, and come to me; hear, that your soul may live.

Without self-consciousness, Priscila expounded on this chapter at length. Her plain, worn face glowed with an inner light as she spoke.

"So many times," she said, "I have been tempted to think like everyone else. But then I go back to these verses."

> "For my thoughts are not your thoughts, neither are your ways my ways," says the Lord. "For as the heavens are higher than the earth, so are my ways higher than your ways and my thoughts than your thoughts" [Isa. 55:8-9].

As Priscila prayed in Luo, and I in English the sun dropped to the horizon. It bathed us in a buttery, warm glow that lay across the open window. The language barriers had dissolved; both of us felt we had understood the essentials. I saw that Priscila had lost her physical strength and grown old. She had no husband, no children. Yet for years Priscila had been investing in another kingdom, where there would be neither hunger nor thirst. She knew where her treasure was.

3. Mariamu—Accused of Witchcraft

Mariamu Kisigiro. Born 1926, Mwikoma tribe, Ikoma, Tanzania.

The small, bare, wood table had been loaded with good food. It had been cooked just for us by the young women who had lounged around the fire in the backyard kitchen all morning. Chicken cooked in sauce, ughali, rice, boiled greens; and for dessert, sweet tea and white bread. We three westerners—Jan, our interpreter; Jill, the local missionary doctor's wife; and I—settled gratefully onto a black Naugahyde settee. It had been a morning of intensive interviewing.

Ludia Mbeba, the motherly national church worker who was conducting these interviews for me, was also a guest. Yet she fit in like a missing relative. Other church women lounged on folding chairs against the mud-plastered walls of their pastor's house, chatting.

Mariamu entered, taller than anyone present. She posed dramatically in the doorway. In a moment of silence she asked, "Do you remember the time when I saw the dead man, Mweta?"

Bill Cosby couldn't have done it better. The women dissolved in giggles, knowing a comedy routine had begun.

Mariamu played it straight, with a grim "why me?" expression as she told about a friend of hers, Mweta, who had come into the hospital to die. As a nurse there, she had warned him about hellfire and urged him to repent, for he was a great rascal. Some days after he had died, Mariamu was walking down a street, minding her own business. Suddenly she saw an apparition of Mweta. He stood some distance off, smiling and waving at her.

"Well, what do you want?" she had barked in fright, not at all glad to see a ghost. "You're dead!"

But Mweta continued to smile and wave, unperturbed. "Since he was smiling, I suppose he had come to tell me that he had taken my advice and escaped hell," Mariamu guessed. Her sour face expressed distaste over what Mweta continued to get away with.

By now the women were howling with laughter. Mariamu's comic timing was perfect, even via Jan's translations.

"You, the one with the ears, sit down," her friends teased her amid their giggles. Mariamu had the long, stretched earlobes with big holes formerly common to her tribe. A woman in the room admitted that she had asked a doctor to cut off her earlobes and sew up the edge so she wouldn't look old-fashioned.

"When I was a child," Mariamu told us Westerners, "there were several growing-up ceremonies. The first was when I was about ten, and I had my ears done. Holes are cut in the lobe and a heavy piece of wood inserted. The weight eventually stretches the ear longer."

"Then when I was about fifteen, I was circumcised."

"Which was worse?" I ask.

Mariamu's face dropped in mock dismay at my stupidity. Amid our laughter, she began a comedy routine on circumcision, the hardest growing-up ceremony.

"Everyone is here, and they are looking at you!" She imitated the pep talk her aunt gave her before the ceremony. "Your uncles are here, your aunts are here. Everyone you know is here. I suppose you are going to shame the family and cry?"

By the time her aunt was done with her, Mariamu needed no one to hold her down. "Go ahead and cut," her macho body language implied. Again the women went into gales of laughter.

I wondered how could we all be laughing about something so grisly. Our hilarity reminded me of Cosby's childbirth routine: "What does it feel like to have a baby?" And his famous line, "Like someone is pulling your bottom lip up over your head!"

But then Mariamu imitated the operation with her hand. A gouging motion to excise the clitoris. Three or four cuts to trim off the large and small labia. My smile died. I knew that circumcised women believe their pubic area is far cleaner and more aesthetically pleasing.

The truth is that the scar tissue that forms is taut and inflexible. It often prolongs labor and tears in childbirth. The scar tissue is also numb, preventing women from feeling many sexual sensations other than pain.

I masked my sadness. My job was to listen, to try to understand.

Circumcision, in its various forms, is often defended by sociologists as the gateway into tribal identity. Dying out among those with more education, it is still practiced vigorously among the tribes who hold onto their heritage, such as the Maasai of Kenya. In other tribes and areas, it was never practiced.

For Africans with Moslem and Arab influence, it is prescribed by the Koran. Some groups simply slice off the clitoris; others excise it completely. Still others go much further and operate on the labia as well. Sometimes they sew the woman's natural opening almost shut.

Circumcision was a type of purification ceremony. Having endured the pain, the girl had proved herself worthy of adult status in the tribe. The next step would be child-bearing.

"I was in severe pain for about eight days," Mariamu remembered nonchalantly. "At the time I couldn't wait to have it done. I wanted to be grown-up, like everyone else, and respected. Those thoughts keep you from feeling the pain."

While my thoughts had been wandering, the party had broken up. The sun had dropped. It was time to go. Women climbed into Jan's van, and we dropped them off reluctantly, one at a time. They sang, trilled joycries, and blessed each other farewell.

The ululation, made by trilling the tongue and shrieking at the same time, never failed to raise gooseflesh on me, and this was no exception. I vowed to go off in a field somewhere and learn how to do it. It felt as though we were coming home from a giant pep rally. No one wanted the day to end.

Mariamu limped out of the van in front of a tiny but immaculate storybook, thatched cottage. Yellow lilies grew in clumps in her dirt yard, the first flowers I had seen outside an African home. A neat, little corral was formed with clumps of dead wood and brush. I remembered that this little property was all hers, achieved with great pride.

This was the story that Mariamu had told me that morning:

"In my girlhood, I was circumcised at about the age of fifteen. Soon after I had healed, my legs began to hurt.

[Mariamu implied a possible causal connection between the circumcision and the onset of bone disease, but this is hard to ascertain. Research does suggest, however, that many complications do accompany these circumcisions, including chronic bladder and uterine infections which may eventually cause sterility.]

"That was the beginning of this disease I've had in my leg all these years.

"The first man who was interested in me worked in Nairobi. He came home and found me here in the Mugumu district which borders on the great Serengeti plain. I was already a bit older than the other unmarried girls; he wanted to take me with him.

"My father accepted ten sheep as a bride-price, but he said, 'I don't want her to go to Nairobi with her hurt leg. Let her stay home until it is healed.'

"So Father took me to a traditional healer who made little cuts and inserted herbal medicines. Three years went by, and the leg went on hurting. Eventually the man in Nairobi got tired of waiting and took his bride-price back. My father died and I went on living at home.

"Then this other man came to ask for me. My mother agreed. Other girls my age already had borne two children. He gave her a small bride-price and I went with him.

"For six years we lived together, and I bore no children. We fought with each other. Sometimes he beat me. He was a husband, wasn't he?"

Mariamu glossed over these six barren years quickly. But I knew as I listened that bearing no children was the worst disaster that could befall a young woman. Her listening friends began to giggle, lightening the mood purposely. "Your husband beat you because you were a fornicator," they said laughing. Even Ludia had to laugh. Mariamu turned her perfect deadpan face on them and then continued.

"Then in the sixth year of my marriage, my sister-in-law gave birth there in our compound. The baby died after four days. The mother, too, became very ill.

"Whose fault was it? In the old days, when someone died or became ill, we usually looked for someone who was jealous or angry as the possible culprit—someone who could have put a spell on them."

I remembered Mister Rogers had assured my children repeatedly that "wishing a bad thing doesn't make it come true." But in Africa, most believed in such strong subconscious powers.

"All eyes in the compound turned on me," Mariamu said. "Because I had no babies of my own, they believed that I was a sorcerer. They accused me of causing the child's death!" Her voice broke, and she waited a moment.

"The worst thing was that my husband joined them in accusing me. We agreed that I should leave. So I went home. Later my husband came to my mother's house and got his bride-price back. I never married again."

Now the tears flowed and Mariamu stopped, remembering the pain of thirty years ago as if it were still fresh. It was a surprise to see this self-mocking comedian, big-boned and controlled, look so crushed.

"Oh, those were difficult years. I became an angry person, a sharp person. I wasn't kind. I was an adulteress. I was a great sinner before God.

"Then in 1955-56, while I was living with my mother, I began taking catechism. Jesus saved me in 1958, and I was baptized at Robonda. I began to see that my life could be different.

"One day I spoke to a missionary who was building churches out in our district. 'Can I come and live at the mission?' I asked him. The mission was several hours away, near Lake Victoria.

" 'Well,' he said, 'let me go back there and ask people.'

"Eventually the mission agreed to let me come and even sent me bus fare. I was to work in an American pastor's home. He already had two cooks there, and I was the third! Because he and his wife didn't have children of their own, they were always taking people in, showing love for others.

"I spent three months there, learning how to do things. Then a single nurse named Velma Eschleman came to visit.

" 'Can I have one of your workers to help me in the clinic?' she asked the pastor.

" 'You just tell me which one you'd like,' the pastor said.

" 'I want this girl,' Velma said, pointing to me.

" 'Oh, don't trouble yourself with her,' the pastor's wife warned her. 'She can't even read yet; she doesn't know anything. Why not take this other girl? She has four years of school already and could start clinic work right away.'

"But Velma was adamant. 'Jesus told me this is the girl I should take with me,' she insisted."

Mariamu's eyes sparkled. She leaned forward in her chair, body erect, as she said, "And she meant me!"

"On January 13, 1960, Velma came and got me. We went to Kisaka Clinic." It was twenty-eight years ago, but Mariamu had not forgotten the date when her call came! "On the eighteenth I started work in the dispensary. I washed wounds and helped the midwives. Later I learned to read a bit, and then I did everything, even gave shots.

"Velma came and went and left things up to me. She would say, 'If the work is too much for Mariamu, then it's too much for me.' In the end, I became a midwife. This is the work Velma called me to and taught me. I worked there for sixteen years, until Velma left.

"During the years at Kisaka I lived in a house on the mission. I took in two newborn babies, a girl and a boy whose mothers had died, and I raised them. [Traditionally, children belong to their clan, no matter who has raised them. Clan members usually felt free to reclaim children at an age when they could be useful. Thus adoption of children by strangers has never been popular here.]

"The girl's family came for her before dowry time. She is Mwikoma, like I am, and she comes to visit me with her children. But we are not close.

"The boy was Luo, and after he finished two years of school, his family came for him. But when he reached his fifth school year, he came back to me, even though by then I had moved to Mugumu. He had hardly any clothes on his back.

" 'They won't pay my school fees,' Luka told me. 'I have no clothes, not even a place to stay.' I felt very sorry for him. I took one cow to market and got him everything he needed—books, clothes, some food.

" 'Now,' I said, 'Go back to that school where you were and study.'

"But in two weeks he was back. 'I'm not going back there!' he said. So I kept him. I entered him in school here and he finished seventh grade." Mariamu concluded her story about Luka with a satisfied nod of her head.

"When Velma left Kisaka, another young person came in her place. My leg was getting worse. It hurt a lot. So I came back to Mugumu District where my brother was a pastor. I used my savings to build a house. I bought a plow and oxen. I had my cattle, and I farmed. My son helped me.

"My son and his wife live with me now. The cattle and oxen are gone to get him a wife. So we are poor, back to where we started." Mariamu laughs with contentment. "But I do have a hoe!" Evidently the joy of seeing her son's family beginning with such hope for the future was worth every penny to Mariamu.

"I have been happy ever since I found Jesus. I was especially happy during those years in Kisaka. I saw my own sins; I saw how God was working. It was a good life."

She began to recite Psalm 23, her favorite Bible chapter. She intoned it dramatically, Mariamu-style, the pauses as heavy with significance as the words themselves. *She's a born actress,* I thought to myself. Four pigeons fluttered around the open window, and the sun sparkled on their purple and green iridescence. Inside, the women were hushed, involved in Mariamu's story.

"I am an evangelist for God," Mariamu said thoughtfully. "I like to spread the gospel and show others Jesus' goodness. I have been chosen to be an elder here at Morotonga. I can't walk much to visit people, but I pray for them at home. I pray for both believers and unbelievers. This is the work God has given me in my heart. I can do this anyplace."

Talents? She repeated my question and thought. "God gave me the power to take care of those adopted children in my home." She and Ludia chuckle at my Western question. There the question was survival, not talents or self-fulfillment, and few people bothered to think in those terms. So she moved into an area she understood better.

"I hope that the rest of my days I'll live a Christian life. Satan can come and get you at any time. He comes at me through my sickness. Satan walks with a stick. I pray I can fight against it.

"I have so much pain in my legs, arms and back, it's hard for me to sleep. Satan tells me, 'If you can get some person to give you the right medicine you'll get well.' Oh, he has many words to say to me about my sickness.

"I know in my heart that there's no way for me to be cured. I have had two operations this year. One wound still hasn't healed. Every time they operate they take out more bone. They want me to come back for another operation soon."

"Has your childlessness affected your faith in God?" I asked.

"God didn't give me children," she said flatly. "I never wanted to force God, to say 'You must give me children! I can't live unless you give me children!' I didn't want to say that to God.

"I believe that any child of God is a child of mine. Even you are my children," she gestures to Jan and me. I thought of the childless missionaries who took Mariamu in and modeled love to her. I wished they could hear her now: "Any child of God is a child of mine."

"For example, when I lived at Kisaka, a school child came to my house every day after school, and I gave him food. I didn't ask, 'Whose is this child?' I just fed the children.

"One day, years later, he came looking for me, asking where I lived. He brought me goods from the market. 'Mother, are you okay?' he asked me. The next morning he took me to the market, and we picked out some nice clothes. He wanted to give me this gift.

"I got these kangas I'm wearing from another young person. A third brought me a piece of cloth, a *kitenge*. I was so happy to see these young people showing me love because I had helped them before."

Mariamu paused, framed by the open window, the breeze gentle on her face. A safety-pin ornament on her peach blouse, patterned kanga skirt, and head scarf—all proclaimed her a woman of substance. Her face relaxed. In the telling of her story she became vulnerable, finally, and she spoke quietly.

"So you see, I love God. I love God even with my leg condition, and I love the church.

"I don't have any other way to do anything."

4. Martha—Misfortune Was a Cloud over Her Head

Martha Maija. Born 1922, Mjita tribe, Kome Butimba, Majita land, Tanzania

Though it was a warm day, Martha Maija arrived at her crowded town church of Bunda swathed in sweater and head scarf. Her voice was faint and wispy. At age sixty-five, she seemed wraith-like, as if most of life had been burned out of her. She described herself, however, as a farmer. This was how she earned her food now that she had retired as a cook.

"If I hadn't had Jesus, my life would have been sorrowful indeed," she told me, exuding gentleness. "But I found joy in the word of God."

Martha's mother and father had separated when she was small. She was raised by a Christian uncle. She had two years of schooling and at age twelve became a Christian. Later her uncle arranged her marriage to a fine young Christian man. The young couple became parents of a baby boy.

Soon after, however, her husband developed a disease with symptoms like epilepsy. Since epileptic seizures are similar to behavior associated with demon possession, the uncle decided he did not want his niece to remain in that situation.

Martha loved her husband. But her uncle, who had fallen from the church and taken another wife himself, refused to let her stay. He took her away and sent back the bride-price. Because the baby traditionally belongs to the husband's clan, he had to stay behind. Although she didn't know it at the time, he was the only child Martha would have.

Sometime later, Martha again married, this time to a fisherman. But he went on an extended fishing trip on Lake Victoria and died there of a fever.

A third time she married. Her husband's brother got into a fight with someone. Her husband went out and tried to stop the two. He was stabbed accidentally and died in 1947.

"I was twenty-five years old and alone. I had had bad luck, and I didn't want to marry again. My Christian sisters also counseled me to stay alone. Those who were not Christians believed I carried my misfortune with me.

"It was a terribly sad time for me. Within five years I had been taken away from my husband and my child. Then I had these other husbands die.

"After I decided I wasn't going to marry again, I went to Jesus. Then I was at peace. At first people are suspicious of widows. They gossip about your behavior. But after they see that you are a good person, they won't say anything any more.

"In 1956 I was called by the church to go to Nyeraro, to the Mara Hills School, to help cook and clean. They wanted a young widow who was free to go work and live there. Later, Pastor Mugando said it was too far from my home. He arranged for me to go to Muremba Girls School to do the same kind of work.

"Some years later, I went to my mother in Shirati to care for her. After my sister came as well, I started to cook at the Shirati Nursing School, and I stayed there sixteen years.

"I was still young, and I really enjoyed working in all these places. When I was sixty, they said the work was too hard for me, I should go home and rest. They gave me four thousand shillings, [about $150], and I had saved money. So I came back here to Bunda and built a two-room house.

"I must get some help from others to farm. My son is just a farmer, and he lives in Majita, so he can't help me much. So now life is harder, because I don't have any cash."

Martha was given gifts by the nursing students when she left Shirati as a token of how much they liked and respected her. She was a cheerful, gentle person, not given to complaining. Her small face was serene and surprisingly without bitterness.

She said, "I've been a widow since I was young until now. Always God has helped me. My life wasn't hard. People were always there to help me, and I got good work to do. I was always involved in the church. Now I am old, and I am just a member. I'm being taken care of well because it is Jesus who takes care of me.

"The Beatitudes are my favorite Scripture. God has given me the gift to know Jesus and to know that nothing is too great for him."

5. Prisca—God Gave Me Those Girls

Prisca Nyabweke. Born 1920, Mkiroba tribe, Bukiroba, Tanzania.

The fifteen-cow bride-price had been paid. So without further celebration the small-boned, teenage girl left home, carrying baskets of flour with her. She stayed with her mother-in-law for a short time, learning what this new family would expect of her.

Then her husband came for her, admiring her smooth young face and bright eyes. He took her to live with his first wife, so she could be further trained in household chores.

The girl, Prisca, was not happy. There was a lot of quarreling and dissension. Her husband waited impatiently for her to become pregnant. When three years had gone by with no births, he was angry. Finally he ordered her to go back home. Her parents would have to return the price he had paid for her.

Prisca returned home to face ridicule from others. A woman who could not bear children had no place in that society. She had no income and no real home. Her heart hardened. Prisca described herself as a "fornicator." She received small presents of clothing and food from men. She had nothing to lose.

One day a well-liked missionary came to visit the twenty-year-old girl. He talked about the Christian faith. But, she said, "I did not *want* to believe!"

Later, however, she attended church services. Her friends still mocked her. "If you become a Christian, where will you get your nice clothes? You have no children. Why don't you make beer to earn your living?"

One night, she had a vivid dream. "Something, formed like a person but not quite a person, and draped in shining white clothes, came into my room. I was aware of this warm presence and it called me, 'Prisca, come to me.'

"I woke up and looked around for this person but realized that the room was very dark. I could not have seen anyone. That same night I accepted Jesus as my Savior."

After that, when Satan brought temptations, like wind blowing over Prisca, she ran to Jesus to pray and to ask forgiveness.

When people laughed at her, she told them that Jesus would take care of her.

Soon afterward, her former husband offered to let her return. Prisca refused. Now she had Jesus.

About this time the local missionaries were opening a four-year school for girls about twelve years old. The Mkiroba were a conservative tribe, not eager to let their children go, especially the boys. But the missionaries visited homes and won their trust. Some of the families agreed to let their girls learn to read and write. Twenty-five young girls enrolled, and the church asked Nyabweke to serve as housemother for them.

She beamed when she remembered those years. "I enjoyed working with the girls. I was saved, so I could plant seeds in their hearts. I was glad to hear them call me 'Mother.' We forgave each other and lived together. Many of the girls eventually became baptized. It was the best time of my life!"

As her confidence grew, Prisca shared her faith with others. She traveled on evangelistic trips, presented her witness, and prayed with people. Her mother and others in her home village came to Christ because of Prisca's testimony. Now she realizes that this ability to witness was one of the gifts God gave her.

After the school closed, Prisca worked in several other mission-related jobs. Later she lived with a series of relatives. Now she is old and in poor health. But she lives in a nephew's busy compound, playing a mathematical game with the children, dropping smooth stones into pockets. Her teeth are gone, one eye rolls, and the other is dimmed with cataracts. A woman came in from her field, hesitated, and gave one manioc root from the basket on her head to Prisca before ambling on. The old woman now depends on others to provide her needs.

Still she beamed as she told about Jesus. "He is my rock. He helps me in all things. When I'm angry, I find peace with him. I can't walk up to the church anymore, but Christ is with me here. I get a few verses, and I pray.

"I do not feel sorrow because I had no children. I always had a place to go—to Jesus. He gave me the children at the school, and it made me happy. 'The Lord is my shepherd, I shall not want,' is one of my favorite verses.

"In the early days, we Christians were on fire. The church was strong. Now there are still some strong Christians but the church is weaker. There is no more excitement. People say, 'We've already seen the church; we know all about it. The church is too strict. You can't marry more wives or drink beer.'

"I believe the church needs to remain strong. If people are doing wrong, the church should stop them from coming to church and being hypocritical. As for witchcraft, I never believed in any of that. My body is earth; it gets sick. No one else can hurt me. My life is to love God only."

As we leave, she graciously offers me the manioc root just given her as a gift. She hobbled painfully with us to the edge of the compound. "We probably won't meet again on this earth," she said cheerfully. "My health is not at all good, and I don't believe I'll be here much longer."

Then she waved both arms in the air and laughed out loud, as if we were both celebrating that fact. "If you hear that Prisca has died, you'll know that I'm sitting up there with God—waiting for the rest of you!"

Her laughter hung in the warm air over me, her arms still raised in triumph, like a benediction.

CHAPTER

The Co-Wives

1. Polygamy

Polygamy is a marriage arrangement by which a man may have more than one wife—but a woman only one husband. It is obvious to women everywhere, whether African or Western, that this is not a fair arrangement.

Many sociologists who have studied polygamy defend it. There is no doubt it has some advantages. For one thing, by some fluke of nature more African women than men survive into adulthood. Some figures show as many as 1.5 women for every male. In a culture where marriage and childbearing are seen as the apex of experience for women, what would happen to the women "left over" if polygamy disappeared?

The problem is intensified by the practice of marrying girls to men ten or more years older than themselves. As the population grows at the bottom, like a pyramid, more young girls appear and the elder men grow scarcer.

In the polygamous home, as it was practiced traditionally, a child grew up with many mothers, one father, and many aunts and uncles. The village was interrelated. Villagers were committed to helping one another survive through a spiderweb of mutual obligations. While this system did not produce or even admire independent spirits, it did create a sense of safety, community, and increased chance of survival should catastrophe fall.

There were other patterns designed to offset the possibility of disasters capable of wiping out a family line. Children were often sent to live with distant aunts or uncles or grandparents for a year at a time. This broadened their horizons or gave them a chance to attend a particular school.

It was wise not to have all one's eggs in the same basket. If a drought and starvation hit one village, it was likely another village would escape. So if tragedy hit one child, having at least one child in another location was a safety net.

If a husband died, the clan was usually willing to provide a substitute—a brother or an uncle. Thus the woman could continue to bear children in her husband's name. She had married the family as much as the individual man. In this way, even death could not cheat the life force of the clan.

Although social customs varied from tribe to tribe, some groups had rigid taboos concerning sexual behavior. Frequently couples were prohibited from intercourse during menstruation, pregnancy, lactation, and after a woman's menopause. These practices obviously protected the woman by lengthening the space between births to two to three years. They also reinforced polygamous patterns. Sexual abstinence might be expected for the nine months of pregnancy plus another two years for nursing a child.

It is hard for Westerners to realize that traditional marriage arrangements were not particularly concerned with sexual attraction. They were concerned with survival of the clan, the tribe. Husbands were not chosen for young girls on the basis of personality.

A father was concerned about the stability of the man's clan. Would the clan stand behind his daughter and her children and help them survive? Thus a rich, old man, to whom many people owed obligations, was a better prospect for a daughter than an arrogant, young upstart. I think of Tevye, of *Fiddler On The Roof,* courting the butcher for his daughter. "At least she'll never go hungry," he says!

A father handed his daughter into a relationship like that between a student and an authoritarian teacher. The two might spend hours each day pursuing mutual goals. But not much real conversation or romance was likely to pass between the two. Rather there would be a distance, created by fear and respect. Rather severe discipline and even punishment would be expected if the student did not live up to her teacher's expectations.

Both husband and wife stood in a strict line of authority, with people above and below them on the ladder. The proprieties were as strictly enforced as those in Buckingham Palace, complete with curtsies, special titles, and greetings appropriate to one's age and rank.

In such a marriage, young girls turned to the other wives and to a circle of friends for companionship. Almost always they had left their own clan behind to live in the husband's home village. Family support was far away.

Such wives worked at chores together, watched each others' children, and squabbled, as sisters do. This was a life close to the edge of survival, where a woman not only produced as many babies as possible but also worked at hard labor from dawn to dusk. In such a life other wives sometimes provided welcome relief from drudgery.

Romance was something sweet and stolen. There were love affairs, of course, as there are in every culture. But they often flourished independently of the nitty-gritty business of marriage.

M. Scott Peck, the often-quoted United States authority on love and spirituality, defines feelings of romance and infatuation as exclusively sexual in nature. He says that love, on the other hand, is a commitment to growth in another. It involves acts of work and of courage as the lover reaches out beyond herself.

In this deeper sense, African women were obviously great lovers. Many, even though they had been abused, spoke of respecting, even loving, their husbands. They missed them, wished they would return, or mourned their deaths. Through sheer hard work and courage they tried to improve the lot of their families, including husbands, children, co-wives, in-laws, and clan.

Both men and women in Africa relish their relationships. They offer warm and open hearts, especially to friends of their own sex. In Africa one is surrounded by friends. Here no one walks anywhere alone. Children never play alone. They usually run in packs of five, ten, or twenty.

Women carry water together, talking and laughing. Men eat and drink together, go off to cities together to look for work, bathe together, and hold hands affectionately. Africans do not like to be alone. They share tiny beds, tiny houses or rooms, crowd into matatus or vans, sit close even outdoors.

Bob and I still chuckle over an incident that taught us this point. One time we shared a guest house with two Tanzanian brothers, big, cheerful men, both over six feet tall. When they left in the morning, we noticed only one of the two single beds in their room had been slept in. Rather than use up more sheets, they slept together in that tiny bed, as no doubt they had always done.

With a friend or one's siblings, one can moan, cry, sing, dance, laugh out loud. One can work, trill joycries, tell stories, and share everything one has.

While this traditional model of clan life seems idyllic in some respects, it was vulnerable to the same quirks of human nature apparent in the West. Older women told me of the fierce competition rampant between wives for the few material goods available.

Whose children would be chosen to go to school? Who got the meat for the cooking pot when there wasn't enough to go around? When one wife got chased away by her angry husband, how did the co-wives treat the left-behind children?

Life among women in these tiny, closed communities and villages was often fraught with tensions and abuses. Most women in polygamous marriages indicated to me that they did not approve of polygamous marriages; each would have preferred to be the only wife. Some expressed strong bitterness that they had no choice in the matter. Others talked about the years of hurt they had endured. Especially for Christian women, who had married thinking their lives would be different, would be Christian, the disillusionment went deep.

This traditional family model, in which the woman had no choices at all, is now dying out. Modern men and women have accepted Christianity for two or three generations now. They have been watching the Western marriage model.

Thirty-five years ago young Christian men first broke tradition by choosing their own wives from Christian girls' schools with the help of missionary go-betweens. These young couples often had idealistic dreams of a new life-style.

Yet it was difficult even for these Christian pioneer men to renounce the old privileges due them, such as wives who would kneel to serve their food and wait to eat the leftovers. And when a wife proved barren, her husband usually capitulated to the inevitable and took a second wife. A childless family was simply unthinkable.

These couples, now middle-aged, still do not touch in public or sit close together. Out of respect the women still do not speak freely in front of their husbands.

Younger couples, however, at least those who live in the city, have moved closer to a nuclear family unit. Women in particular yearn for the kind of consideration they see in Western marriages.

Men are ambivalent. They are interested in women who seek to be companions to them. Yet they hesitate to renounce their old male privileges. Christianity gives something new to the women. It takes privileges away from the men. It is not surprising that the churches hold more women than men, nor that women have more staying power. Still, college students are fond of saying to their girlfriends, "I want my wife to be my companion, someone who thinks for herself."

In a 1974 study among the Luo tribe of Western Kenya and Tanzania, the site of most of my interviews, 54 per cent of the adults participated in plural marriages. That figure is probably a bit lower by now.

But polygamy is still in the man's best interest there. Men of power and wealth usually take more young wives. It enhances their prestige, both locally and in wider political circles—in all circles, that is, except the church. The young wives are status symbols. What middle-aged or older man wouldn't enjoy having a teenage wife to serve food to his colleagues?

They bring more children—a tie to the future and indeed to eternity. A man might have to die sometime, but all those children will carry his blood and be a continuation of him in some vague way. They are a hedge against death and decay.

Wives are also efficient producers, especially if driven by competition. Usually they manage to raise enough food to feed their offspring and a bit extra. The extra, of course, belongs to the husband.

Old wives are not cast off, as they are in the divorce-prone West. That would be cruel. No, the first wife is still the boss among the younger wives, who must obey her. She may have lost a husband's attentions. But, in theory at least, she retains her prestige, her position, and her security in old age. This is especially true if she has borne sons to provide for her financially.

If the first wife objects too vehemently to junior wives, the husband may desert her entirely, as happened to Hellen and Zipporah (whose stories are told in this chapter). This devastates most women. Given the matriarchal strength of African women, along with their physical strength and endurance, it always puzzled me to hear their often repeated sentiment that they needed their husbands and suffered terribly when the husband died or left.

Women who had been beaten, like Zipporah, or treated badly, told me the same story. They wanted their husbands back. This may be due to the loss of status and self-respect they experience in a society which stigmatizes women living without men. (In the country, it is not unusual for the husband to be absent; he is usually holding a job in the city, and able to visit only several times a year. There is no social stigma attached to his absence, as long as he still holds the family authority in his name.)

A second reason is that a woman alone usually depends on her farming to provide for her family. And this is a precarious means of survival, given droughts, rains, insects, and lack of fertilizer and irrigation. Women alone live on the edge without any safety net. When things go badly, their children go hungry.

A women alone tends to yearn for the automatic respect that she used to receive as "so-and-so's wife," a role which implied adult status. Now her status is gone. Other women eye her suspiciously as a temptation to their own husbands. Men leer. Brothers are annoyed at the implied responsibility they feel. Children come home asking for school fees and books.

Socialized as she has been, interdependent with others all her life, independence is painful and lonely. She must make all the decisions. But when there is no one to lean on, what does a woman do? She learns to stand alone.

Many tribes customarily assume that once a woman reaches menopause, she changes status. She is something between a man and a woman. Indeed, it is easy to notice the freedom of manner and speech of the older woman, her joking repartee. This is not typical of the shy young mother, whose eyes are cast down in mixed company, and who is not to speak when men are present.

Many tribes suggest that sexual relations should no longer take place after a woman's menopause. It is not unusual for men to take new wives then. It is during this period, however, that older women achieve their highest status. They learn to say what they like. They become preachers; they become evangelists; they branch out.

As I talked to women who lived in polygamous relationships, I began to understand more about the entire culture. It was not a cruel culture. Rather, individual rights of all people, both men and women, usually took a back seat to communal survival.

But now, in these transitional times, the old African culture must give way and is changing quickly. Now the women who are caught in the change must find their own ways through. There are no easy answers. Because of the human emotions involved, it is hard to predict what will happen. Even events that seem ordinary can break the heart.

Sixty-seven-year-old Julia Thadayo, well dressed and energetic, received me in her neat home. She was reticent by nature, a woman of action, not words. She let me know in her own way, however, that her husband had broken her heart when he brought home another wife.

"Mine was the first Christian wedding in Shirati, Tanzania," she said smiling. "The missionary bishop married us in 1935, when I was fifteen.

"During the first fifteen years of our marriage, I was very happy. My husband was an elder in the church, and we were both leaders there. Of twelve children born to us, eight are still living. My children are all Christians.

"I could see that my husband's spiritual life was getting cool. Suddenly, he had a second wife. He brought her home to live in the same house.

"He never asked me, never brought it up. And a Luo wife is not supposed to complain. What a man chooses to do is his business.

"He owned a milk separator and many cows. So he had the money to take another wife. But there were big differences between myself, my husband, and the other wife. There was no understanding between us. From then on, I wasn't happy anymore, except for Jesus.

"During those years I continued to teach Sunday school. I would use big pictures to teach the children about Jesus. I didn't let my troubles take me away from my faith.

"I don't agree with polygamy! To have a good marriage, it is better to have only one wife. The two have more in common, and the husband will stay closer to Christ. I believe that for a man to come close to Christ, he would have to leave his second wife.

"To have a good marriage, I would tell young women, 'Really know the Lord, first. Never agree to a second wife. Love your husband—respect him. Love his family, and welcome guests, so that he is proud.'

"After the children of both families were grown, my husband came back to me again. We talked together more. My son built this nice house for me in 1978. He also built a smaller one for his father, so that he would have a place of his own. When my husband died, I felt I had lost him twice. Through all this the Lord taught me to rely on him."

Another church leader, Rachel Igira, a fifty-year-old widow, who had a warm Christian marriage herself, said, "Women have a big problem with their men. Some are drunkards, they marry many wives, and then they don't provide for their children.

"The government is pushing planned parenthood," she said. "But men want lots of children. Some women want birth control. But look at a man who has three wives. Each wife wants the most children—it is like a contest to show whom he loves most. So they go on having children without the money to care for them. In Tanzania a man has to sign a paper for his wife to obtain birth control methods.

"Divorce is better than polygamy," Rachel said in disgust,

"because the women do not have to live with each other. In a polygamous home, there is no peace. There is constant tension. The man is bringing about constant war, so how can he be right with God?

"Oh, co-wives get along all right if it is an old man who no one wants anyway. Or if the women have given up hope of any economic help from the man. Then the wives form an independent economic unit. They band together to help each other. They often father their children outside the marriage. What can we do? Women are helpless about polygamy."

As you will see in the following stories, women may feel helpless about polygamy and other unjust social structures. But they still try to find fulfillment in life. And they do.

Why do young women agree to become junior wives? Rosa and Miriam are the young women who chose to enter a polygamous marriage because they felt they had few other options.

Esther was forced into her arranged marriage as a young girl. Anna is the wife who must make way for seventeen junior wives, although her husband is so violent that she hardly cares. Hellen and Zipporah are senior wives who are openly angry and jealous about their husbands' young wives.

I continue to be overwhelmed by older women like Esther and Anna. They respond to a hard life by developing an inner core of such depth and beauty that those around them continually speak of it. These women have a lot to teach me.

For some months, as I listened to these women, I pondered the meaning of endurance as practiced in these polygamous marriages. Obviously these African women believed that endurance itself was a training ground that would produce higher qualities in a woman. Ear stretching, circumcisions, teeth removal—these exercises in endurance were all meant to teach young women to throw themselves into pain, into the fight for survival, and to win. The lesson was that there was something noble beyond the pain.

But later, as the stories sank deeper into my heart, I began to see that the stories were not about endurance at all. The theme was that at some point God would enter the picture and transform the pain, the struggle. God's love would fill the person and make her transparent. Then one no longer saw the struggle, one saw the love of God.

So I remind myself that polygamy is not the issue of this chapter, any more than divorce is the issue for North American women. The social problem is the backdrop for the struggle. In the foreground are Christian women, showing us how to transform pain into transparent love.

2. Anna—The First of Eighteen Wives

Anna Masrori Sobu. Born 1931, Bantu tribe, Muhoro Bay, Kenya.

Anna Sobu had husband troubles again. No one knew where she was. "Her husband has thrown her out," people told us. "Maybe she is staying with her eldest son, Samson."

I had heard about Anna ever since I had arrived in Kenya. For forty-five years she had not wavered in her faithfulness to Christ. She had been baptized as a young girl at Kirongwe, Tanzania, one of the earliest Mennonite mission stations. Later she had experienced the great East African revival in the 1940s. "That's the reason she's still a Christian," affirmed her friend Bishop Kisare. "She took Jesus into her heart during that revival."

When Anna moved to Kenya, the church moved with her. At her frequent encouragement, a church was planted in her community. She faithfully nourished it.

"You must talk to Anna," Kenyan Christians told me. "Her husband is a rich and powerful man. Yet her life has not been easy. She is one of eighteen wives!"

I would talk to her if I could just find her, I thought. Muhoro Bay, her town, was an outpost at a seldom-used Kenya-Tanzania border crossing, one most favored by smugglers. Given the state of the roads and rumors of thieves, Westerners didn't just drop by there. They had to plan their expedition carefully. There were no phones to deliver messages.

Word came back to me by the incredible African grapevine: "She's not at her son Samson's house, either." I had no choice but to trust that intangible communication system.

"I'm going down to Tanzania for a month," I told people. "Then I will return here. I'd like to see Anna Sobu. If she finds her way to me by bus, I'll gladly reimburse her travel expenses." I even deposited a few dollars with a church worker toward that possible miracle.

Three days later, as our family settled into a guest house near the mission station at Shirati, Tanzania, the bishop sent us a message: "Anna Sobu is here. She heard that you wanted to see her."

"How did she get here!" I gasped, knowing the complex travel and passport arrangements we had gone through.

"She footed it." The messenger shrugged. "She has a brother here in Shirati, and she had to find somewhere to go."

This woman in her mid-fifties had walked over twenty miles in the heat, through barren country, to get here—to what I later discovered was her hometown. By road, it had been a grueling, three-hour ride.

Without a doubt, Anna had been a beautiful girl. Even now, her body stretched by bearing eight children, her face was young and her smile brilliant. She had high cheekbones and a proud, long-limbed posture. Like most older members of her tribe, she was missing the six front, bottom teeth that had been removed ceremonially as a rite of passage to adulthood. Anna wore a ruffled purple and white polyester dress, a yellow-flowered kanga, and a bright head scarf.

The interview was difficult as conversation was interpreted from Luo to Swahili to English. But I could tell that, despite her colorful outfit, this woman was suffering from depression.

"My husband has chased me away. This time I know it is for good," she said. "He chased me away three other times, but when he needed me for something, he called me back. But this time it is permanent. My fourteen-year-old son Samuel is still at home. That was hard, leaving him, but I know that he will be all right." Her dispirited tone of voice hinted that Samuel still needed her in spite of her words and the custom which gave custody of all Luo children to the father.

"I want to build a small house here in Shirati. The mamas in the church will help me get an allocation from the town. [Land there is communally owned, and the town elders would allot space for a house and some field area for farming, although that might be quite far outside of town.]

"I want to start a small business. I could walk to the lake and buy fish, and then smoke it and sell it at the market. Or I could bake *mendozzis* [fried bread] for the market. My husband will not help me. I have nothing. But I believe I can get by."

Anna's words were brave. But her posture spoke of mental exhaustion. Her voice was lethargic. I knew she had worked hard all her life. Having to start life over and build up a small business to feed herself was indeed daunting. She was elderly by African standards.

Her voice picked up enthusiasm and her eyes gained luster as she continued. "Some of my friends advise me to go to court to gain some of my husband's wealth. They tell me that of all the wives, I helped my husband's business the most. But as a Christian, I won't sue. For me that would be sin. My wealth is in heaven. God will supply my needs!"

Slowly Anna told her story. She sat in a reed chair, legs akimbo under the long flowered kanga, muscular, thin arms resting on her knees.

Anna's father had arranged her marriage through a mutual acquaintance. Neither she nor her family knew Sobu, but he was an ambitious young man who owned a small *duka* (shop) and a sewing machine. Those credentials plus a hefty eighteen-cow dowry were enough. At age seventeen, the pretty young girl left home to become a first wife.

One and a half years later, as Anna gave birth to their first son, Sobu brought home a second wife. This was hardly unusual. Traditionally couples were expected to abstain from sexual relations while a woman was pregnant or nursing. But soon he brought two more. Family life grew chaotic. Sobu was a fierce man, given to beating his wives with any stick or furniture he could grab.

"We wives lived in fear because he was so unpredictable. One minute he was cheerful. The next he was furious. I never knew what he wanted or how I was failing. Every time one of my children made a mistake, I was blamed.

"I never suffered for food or clothes. But life was full of conflict," said Anna. "When I was young, I used to run away and go to my parents, but they would always take me back.

" 'This is your rightful place,' they told me. You see, they had 'already eaten the cows.' [This is the local expression for spending the money derived from the cows.]

"Eventually Sobu married 18 wives. If he saw a woman he wanted, he took her without paying cows. So there was nothing to hold her. She would run away or he would chase her off. Women were always coming and going. When I left there were thirteen others on the compound. Of course, even though the women left, their children had to stay behind," Anna explained.

"As first wife, I tried to establish as much peace as I could. I wasn't jealous. I welcomed the women, and they came to me for advice. I worked in the shop. The other women cooked and did chores together. They respected me. I was responsible for them, and they obeyed me. If both women are soft-hearted, co-wives can get along well."

Anna learned to read a bit as an adult in a bush school offered by a missionary. Her husband trusted her because she was a Christian and gave her the money to save. She continued to help him in the shop and was clever at saving small sums of money. Their business grew. She remained active in the church as well.

Anna gave birth to eight children. One died in childbirth. Her second son, Joni, was killed in a tragic accident at age twenty-one. Her husband didn't allow the children to acquire much education except for Noah, the third son, who proudly finished grade seven.

Today Anna takes great pride in her three sons and three daughters. Samson, her eldest son and the traditional caretaker of his parents, is estranged from his father. "But he is a fine Christian man," she said.

When the family moved across the border to Kenya, the businesses continued to grow. Soon Sobu was one of the wealthiest men in the district.

Anna Sobu, still a staunch Christian, campaigned to open a Mennonite church in her new and undeveloped area. Sure enough, church leaders were sent to plant a church. Anna was an active leader and a children's teacher. She attended district meetings faithfully. She liked to accompany evangelistic teams to other villages to tell her testimony.

Sometimes Sobu cheerfully invited church leaders to his compound for meals. Other times he would fly into rages, and seeing how much Anna loved her church, he would forbid her to attend. Then she would sit at home until he cooled down again.

Finally other church members suggested to Anna that she open a small church at home rather than walk the six kilometers to Muhoro Bay and risk her husband's wrath. So she began preaching each week to the other Sobu wives and one other family. She called her small group Tagatch Mennonite Church. She loved it.

She discovered that God had given her the talent to be an evangelist and preacher. " If I were free," she said smiling, "that is what I'd love to do. That's why I'm living on this earth, to tell others about the Lord." Her face lights with pleasure as she describes this little church.

Her favorite text is Luke 5:20, which focuses on Jesus' words, "Your sins are forgiven you. . . ."

"Follow Jesus. Believe in him. Leave your sins behind you, " she tells the worshipers.

A gentle, thoughtful woman, Anna has depended greatly over the years on her fellow Christians and their counsel. "It is because of their counsel and my own faith that I stayed with my husband," she says. "It wasn't only my children that kept me there. Many women run away and leave their children. No, it was God."

Anna's husband's worst tantrum occurred a few years ago. Going into a rage over some slight oversight of hers, he grabbed her Bible and songbooks and threw them into the fire. "Those Christians have ruined you," he shouted, "and I want them out of my village."

With that he shut down the tiny but precious Tagatch congregation over which Anna presided. He invited a Pentecostal group to meet in the building instead.

Anna mourned the loss of this church. It represented God's calling out of her gifts as well as a real spiritual comfort. Now she was homeless as well.

"Could you live with Samson?" I asked. "Yes," she said with a shrug. "But my husband will say that I have become my son's wife and turn it into something bad. I think it will be better if I build my own house. Life will be peaceful.

"I am not angry or fighting anymore," she said with sorrow, her work-worn hands clasped quietly. "My husband could have been a good man, but Satan ruined anything that could have been. I still love and respect my husband—I do not wish him any harm. I am at peace. I leave my life in God's hands and accept what God brings me."

For a Bantu-Luo woman, marriage is forever. It even extends past her husband's death. Although her life has been hard, it doesn't change the fact that she is Sobu's wife. If he summons her to come home, she says she will return—even though life alone would be immeasurably easier. She endures what she cannot change, though the enduring has never been easy and her life has obviously been deeply sad.

Anna is a traditional woman. She has done the best she could with the circumstances God gave her. She said, "Jesus lives in me. I live in Jesus. I won't return to the world."

In Shirati, Anna is again enveloped in the warm embrace of a large congregation. She is well known and the women there are a great comfort to her. "I learned to know God through the Mennonites," she says. "It's like my own house. I don't know other houses. I will die in my own house!"

Anna's husband, Sobu, died several months after this interview.

3. Esther—The Reluctant Bride

Esther Werema. Born 1942. Mkiroba tribe, Nyansaraba, Tanzania.

Cheerful voices and fragments of laughter floated down the path from the women up ahead. They ambled at the same deliberate pace they always used when walking to their fields.

But today they did not carry fifty-pound loads on heads or backs. Today the women's Bible meeting was going to a member's house for worship.

The path angled out of the village, up the hillside. We stayed on the bare earth footpath, watching for snakes and struggling over deep ruts eroded by rain gullies. We passed carefully weeded maize and groundnut fields, all handworked by the women farmers, and occasional thatch huts surrounded by goats and children.

As we climbed, I kept hanging back to drink in the view. From this elevation, Lake Victoria shone silver, ringed by pale violet hills on the far shore. The lake nestled among rolling, green-brown hills like those we climbed, fertile yet threatened by capricious droughts.

"Droughts? Next to one of the largest lakes in the world?" I questioned this with typical Western density.

Ludia, our intelligent host and interpreter, would only shrug. "We don't have machinery here."

Missionaries had already explained to me the various irrigation schemes begun here in the past fifty years. Most worked until parts broke down or bits of pipe were stolen. Foreign currency was needed to order new parts. This was hard to get because Tanzanian currency was useless outside the country. So most things stayed broken. Without complaint, women resumed carrying water on their heads. Missionaries would always conclude, "The simplest, most natural methods, those easiest to maintain and repair, are best in development." It became a litany.

Above us, huge chunks of yellow, bare rock, natural sculptures, capped the top of the hill. White masses of clouds filled the immensity of space.

The group members, strung out in twos and threes for conversation, waited for each other now and walked up to a quiet hut. They called the usual greeting. "Hodi!" The door opened on smiling husband, children, relatives—all there to celebrate a new baby.

The group leader went in to pray with the mother and leave a gift of food. The baby was brought out and thrust into my arms. He had soft, black ringlets, creamy, light skin, and a round, alert face. I prayed that this child would live. I tried not to think about the diarrhea, measles, and respiratory infections he would need to fight later to be one of the five in ten babies who survive.

The path continued up and wound sideways around the hill. We were heading for Esther's compound to comfort her co-wife, who had lost a small child to illness a week earlier.

The compound consisted of neat mud-walled houses built close together, surrounded by carefully swept dust courtyards. Small fruit and shade trees, with songbirds dipping in and out; a green *shamba* or garden; and the muted colors of Lake Victoria below, shimmering in the distance—all gave the place a peaceful, Garden-of-Eden tranquillity. *I could be happy living here*, I told myself. Except that here small children died, and their mothers grieved.

Palm leaf shade branches were laid flat on upright poles, shading fifteen folding chairs. The chairs had probably been hand-carried from the church. The women, in their brightly colored and patterned kangas, swept into the chairs like a flock of beautiful birds, subdued by the occasion.

We got out our hymnbooks and began singing familiar melodies with African shading and Swahili words. "Tis so sweet to trust in Jesus," which became "Kumtegemea Mwokozi." Or "What a friend we have in Jesus," which became "Yesu kwetu ni rafiki."

One of the women had prepared some remarks and referred to her Bible often. The women left a small gift of money. But it was easy to see that it was the visit itself, the presence of the women, that lifted the middle-aged woman up in her grief. These women had walked to her compound and were blessing her with their prayer and total attention, a rare event.

An ancient man, almost blind and with parchment skin, made a speech to welcome us. The speech was only partly in touch with the occasion. He was treated with respect. Esther acted as hostess, for it was she who had invited her group to come. Even though she was the junior wife, it was obvious that her gentle stateliness made her the natural leader in the home. She bade all the women a gracious farewell.

It wasn't until the next day that an interview with Esther alone had been arranged. When she came to Ludia's house to meet me, she had a list of excuses. She had many things to do that day and could only stay a short while. I could see she was shy and uncomfortable with the focus on her.

As we prayed together, and I shared my goals, Esther slowly allowed herself to relax. With elbows balanced on her wide open knees, with somber profile, thin, brown arms in sharp angles to her purple kanga skirt, she presented a lyrical African portrait of a "lady." It was a pose I had seen on so many lovely batiks—the dye paintings popular with tourists.

She spoke softly, hesitantly. Ludia was conducting the interview, with Jan translating quietly for me. As all three of us listened, Esther began to tell her story, an incident at a time, as if puzzled as to why we would show interest in her.

"When I was young," she began, "I had the gift of gentleness. The clan said I had inherited my nature from my grandmother. When we girls slept in the girls' hut, the others would sneak out at night for adventures. But I didn't. I had attended four years at a nearby primary school and had been baptized. I was young, but I was serious about wanting to follow Jesus.

"When I was sixteen years old, my father announced my marriage arrangements. Everyone was shocked. I would be sent to an eighty-five-year-old cousin, a non-Christian, as a fifth wife. The old man had a business buying and selling cows and ran a cream separator. In our village eyes, he was rich. He was willing to pay thirty-seven cows!"

Esther kept her eyes on the floor, her long, brown fingers weaving together nervously as she remembered her marriage. "I was afraid. I was forced into this marriage and didn't know what to do. I knew that neither my husband nor any co-wives were

Christians. I feared most of all that this husband would not permit me to attend church, and I would be cut off from the fellowship of Christians. Later I got the courage to ask his permission. He agreed that I could go. I just praised God!

"Life was still difficult, however. The first wife was angry and jealous of me. And I thought, *Why should I be married to this old man!* Before I had children, I thought a lot about running away. But I knew that all those cows were gone. They had been used to arrange my brothers' marriages. It would have been considered terrible to leave without returning the bride-price. I had to stay.

"After a time, I decided that I'd make the best of it and show that I could be a Christian even in this. Saying words means nothing if you don't have actions to go with it. So I started to show others the life of Christ, and they responded."

Hesitantly, in her low voice, Esther continued. "I didn't go to dances, drink beer, or exchange bad words with people. The common way is for co-wives to live as enemies. But with my co-wives, I showed love, as though we were sisters. When I have food, and another wife doesn't, I share. Even now, when I cook, I invite all the children to eat. Christ can fill us with love instead of hatred, so that everyone can be our friends and sisters.

"I began to know real joy in my life. As my eight children were born, I felt better about my situation. I saw that Jesus was the value in my life.

"The first wife came to love me. She was happy for me to do her field work. She acted as grandmother to my children. Even today my children are close to her and call her Bibi, which means 'grandmother.'

"We are all troubled by so many things. But we don't have to hate or feel jealous if someone has something we don't have. We don't have to resent serving when someone else has invited a guest. When we walk in the light, we feel welcoming, close, friends with everyone."

As Esther described her life in relational terms, I thought about her day-to-day life. In a Tanzanian village, a woman works from morning until night. There is water to carry, firewood to gather, fields to cultivate, flour to grind. Producing food and nurture for eight children is a monumental task. Yet Esther had obviously managed to find time to nurture others as well.

Two of Esther's co-wives have accepted Christ and been baptized. By 1972, Esther's witness had helped prepare Nyangi Warioba, her husband, and the first wife for baptism. Since polygamy would have kept the old man from being baptized in Esther's church, the couple entered the Catholic Church. (Policies concerning polygamy differ in the various local congregations, although most refuse communion and leadership responsibilities to polygamous men. Women are assumed to be innocent, since they often had little say in their marriage arrangements.)

Esther's mother and her brothers—the ones who had been only too eager to use the cows she brought to the family—have also come to Christ.

"I speak to the children of my co-wives, too," Esther continued. "One young woman said to me, 'If I become a Christian, I will be a fool!'

" 'Yes,' I replied to her, 'people think we are crazy for being happy even though people do bad things to us. Try the way. See if you think it is foolishness. Learn the catechism, be baptized, and see.'

"Later the young woman became a Christian and came back to me.

" 'I spoke rudely to you for such a long, long time,' she told me. 'You always answered me kindly and patiently. finally I was ready to follow your advice. Now I see how hard the Christian life is.'

"When I see someone walking in sin I feel sorrow at such a waste of life. I don't hesitate to visit and say 'There's a way to stop bitterness in your life!' "

Esther's voice became more animated. She smiled as she remembered changed lives. "Sometimes I see a woman who has children and is drinking too much. I wait until she is sober. Then I counsel her, 'Sister, if you could leave this beer and follow Jesus you'd have a better life.' I want her to be saved and to find some reason for living. I want to share my joy in Christ with others."

"You are a midwife, too, aren't you?" Jan interrupted.

"Yes, but I don't charge anything." Esther shrugged. "I volunteer if I am needed. Sometimes people need food or medicine; then I try to provide it."

Ludia laughed. "We have a nickname for Esther. We call her 'Mama Haruna.' " [There is a government welfare office called Bwana Haruna.]

"Last year, Esther was sent to her church district meetings," Jan recalled. "She was the only woman delegate there. Even though she is so quiet, she spoke up frankly. She disagreed with church officials. This is rarely done by those caught up in church politics. However, this gave others the courage to deal openly with the issue and resolve it. I was really impressed with her."

Esther shifted in her chair, stood up, and retied her kanga at the waist. When she resumed her eyes were sad. "I have struggles, too. Struggles I need to bring to God. My eldest daughter began having spells. She became incoherent and her arms and legs would shake. The local doctor told me it was a traditional illness and recommended a traditional doctor. [These spells, which are not uncommon in Africa, have often been associated with demon possession. They are treated as such by the traditional doctors.] I took her to Bunda to see this man. Instead of helping, he seduced her.

"Oh, I was angry and grieved. I prayed and prayed for my daughter. She elected to stay with this 'husband' and continued to have seizures. I knew he wasn't treating her well.

"My advice to my children is always 'Come to God!' One can't force it. We must wait and hope. It's a little like digging in a hard place. One goes slowly, slowly, with great patience and eventually one succeeds.

"After the births of two children, my daughter returned to live with me. After fervent prayer in the church she has returned to God and has improved greatly. Sometimes the elders prayed with her every day.

"My husband is over 116 years old now and still lives quietly on the compound. [It was he who had greeted our prayer meeting there.] There are over thirty children and his herds have been scattered to provide marriages for the sons. The sons are now responsible for the old one's support and other clan members bring him things.

"The other wives and I each have a small herd of cows. I milk eight cows. That provides me with the money I need for school fees and my family. I still have four school-age children at home; they help me in our large shamba that we use to grow our own food.

"I have good children. The boys don't come to the church like the girls do. But they don't drink and are good people. Boys are much harder to raise.

"We get many guests in our compound," Esther said. "Sometimes people come to visit. My husband is the oldest man and elder of the Mkiroba tribe. He's a living history book and knows all about the customs of long ago. I try to greet these guests with hospitality. I think about 1 Corinthians 13, my favorite Bible chapter.

"Faith, hope, love . . . and the greatest of these is love. This, " she said, "is the key. That is what has helped me live successfully in a difficult situation. Love."

4. Rosa—Demon-Possessed No More

Rosa Penina Hamisi. Born 1960, Mjita tribe, Ruwanga, Majitaland, Tanzania.

Rosa had a sweet face, young and innocent. Her baby, Lucia, age one, sucked on her full breasts as we talked. Occasionally Rosa would tuck her breast back into the black skimpy bra and try to pull her blouse closed. But it was a futile maneuver. Her body was too full for the wornout clothing. She was beautiful; her smile lit up her whole face, like a child's.

"When I was saved two years ago," she told me, "I had a *jinni*. [This is the Moslem term for an evil spirit.] I was very frightened. I would get very cold and start to tremble. My back would hurt. I would start crying all of a sudden. Then my arms and legs would dance.

"I thought it was some illness, but my husband took me to see a Moslem traditional doctor who specialized in *mijinni*. I was there for two days. The doctor played the drums for a long time.

He wanted the spirits to respond to the drums and speak out—admit who they were.

"My body responded to the drums. It felt good all over and stopped hurting. But the spirits didn't speak. The doctor was going to give me some medicine to make them come out, but my own spirit told me this was not the right way. I decided to go to Kabara instead, where there is a Pentecostal pastor who also is known for working with demons.

"My father lives in Kabara, so I went there. I arranged a time with the pastor and the deacon, and at four in the afternoon I came to the pastor's house.

" 'Have you really decided to be prayed for?' the pastor sternly asked.

" 'Yes, that is what I want to do.'

" 'And your father has agreed?'

" 'Yes.'

" 'You have decided to put yourself in God's hands to be healed?'

" 'Yes.'

" 'Then kneel down. You will say a few words before God.'

"I repeated the words, 'Mungu, God, please forgive me all the sins I have done. I put myself in your hands. I submit myself to you.' "

"We three Christians took out the songbook, sang, prayed, and the pastor taught for a short time from the Scriptures. Then the pastor asked me to sit before them on the floor. They sang a song for me. Suddenly, I felt something and began to cry. The jinni, the spirits, came out and showed themselves.

" 'Who are you?' the pastor asked.

"But the spirits would not speak. I went on crying.

" 'In the name of the Lord, I don't want to hear crying; I want answers,' the pastor shouted. 'Who are you! How many of you are there?'

"My hands were fists. 'Be gone!' the pastor commanded. But I shook my head no. It was the spirits doing that, not me.

" 'In the name of Jesus Christ, be gone!'

"My fists relaxed. I put my hand up as though to wave goodbye. Five had left. There were five spirits remaining.

"So the pastor went on repeating his commands. He knew they weren't all gone. Finally four more left. Now one remained. It was the big one, the one in my back. The pastor kept praying and telling it to leave. I kept shaking my head.

" 'By the blood of Christ, you must leave this woman. She is not yours, she belongs to God. Tell me your name.'

"From my throat, a low rough voice answered, 'Abdullah.'

" 'How long have you stayed in this woman's body?'

" 'Three years.'

"Then the pastor closed his eyes and prayed with force. 'You must leave. This body is not yours,' he insisted.

"I got down on my hands and knees and retched, like I was vomiting something that had to come out with such force. Then I sat back, and stopped crying.

"He put me on a chair and began to pray again. 'Now you must believe that God has healed you. There must be no doubt about it,' he said.

"So I went to my father's house. Every day I came back to the house in the evening, and the pastor would pray for me. I knew that Satan wanted to tempt me again. I found that my legs were numb, and my back hurt again. But the pastor told me, 'This is a temptation of Satan. If you stand firm in the faith, Satan will not be able to enter you.'

"Two years have gone by now. I have not had those problems again. I know God healed me. I keep asking God to go on healing and teaching me.

"I know in my heart that I am saved and that God loves me. But even Christians do not always understand this.

"One day, soon after I was healed, at the time of giving thanks in church, I stood up. All of a sudden I was overwhelmed with my own sins; I began to cry. Right there I got on my knees and prayed that God would forgive me.

"Some people said to each other, 'Look, she has so many sins, she has to cry.' Others said, 'Oh, lots of people started out strong. She'll soon leave it, too. Look at all her friends, committing adultery. She'll never keep it up.' And some said, 'You shouldn't speak in church like that until you've built a strong base. Then people will respect what you have to say. Too many others spoke like that and then left.'

"The only thing I felt then was that I wanted God to forgive those people. I knew that God had given me the words I spoke. They were authentic. I prayed that Satan wouldn't enter into this.

"A year later, the elders wanted to choose someone to do volunteer work in the church clinic. And even though my husband is not a Christian and I have small children, they asked my husband if he would permit me to do this work. He said, 'Of course. She loves Jesus. If she wants to do this I won't stop her.'

"The elders chose me, and this told me that now they had accepted that my faith is real. I love the work at the clinic. I go there several days a week and farm on the other days."

"Are evil spirits often a result of sin?" I asked Rosa.

She thought for awhile, but obviously didn't see any connection, at least in her own life. "I just thought I was sick," she explained shrugging.

"Tell me about your family," I urged Rosa as little Lucia tugged again at the full breast. We were sitting under a shade tree in the pastor's courtyard. Goats and chickens wandered by, amusing Lucia. From time to time Rosa set the bare-bottomed baby down on a new patch of dry ground because she had diarrhea. It always amazed me that African babies sat where they were put, making little attempt to crawl off. They were used to backslings and mother's heartbeat and breast. They seemed contented with life.

"My husband is Mswaga Mginira," she began. "Well, we've never had a marriage ceremony. He still hasn't paid the bride-price. My parents ask for it, and his parents still say they are trying to find the cows. They have had many problems and have no cows.

"He courted me, and I became pregnant. I was seventeen. After I had my baby, I decided it would be best to stay with him. He already had a first wife and six children. Now we have four living children together.

"When I had my first child by him, I had been baptized. But I was not really a Christian yet. He too had studied catechism but had not accepted Christ. That is one of our problems. I keep asking him to come to church. He keeps saying that he will, but he doesn't. As problems come up, I counsel him that Jesus can help him.

"His first wife brews beer, and he helps her. They serve the beer to guests; that brings them some income. He likes her better than me now because they make money. If he became a Christian, he would lose this income.

"There is no love between his first wife and me. We live in two separate compounds. When I was healed of evil spirits, though, I came back and wanted to be reconciled with her. 'Let's get rid of the bad feelings between us,' I said to her. She agreed, but she doesn't have the same love in her heart that I do. Sometimes she even refuses to greet me. So our relationship is still not strong.

"When I became a real Christian, I went to the church, and I asked what I should do. I was a second wife, after all. Should I leave my husband?

"But they said, 'You have these five children. What will you do? People will think you are running around. In your situation, it would be better to stay with the children's father.'

"I would like to be at peace with everyone. Our time here is short. I believe the things we are seeing are the end times. So I don't want to look at things of the world but at God. I learned this when my child died."

It was hard to imagine that Rosa had had five children. She looked like a child herself. Of the five, only one had been a boy—four-year-old Nyamweko. He had gotten sick.

"I took my songbook," said Rosa, "and I was singing and praying for my son. I was joyful. I thought the child would soon get better. Then my heart told me to take the Bible and read I Peter 4:12. There I found 'Beloved, do not be surprised at the fiery ordeal which comes upon you to prove you. . . .'

"Then I wanted to pray. As I prayed, the words of Jesus 'Let the little ones come unto me. . .' came to my mind. I knew it was in the Bible but didn't know where. I opened the Bible and there it was, on the open page.

"I was peaceful. I knew God had given me those verses. He was with me. But I also began to see that my baby was going to die. So many thoughts came to me. How could I lose my boy child?

"My husband suggested that I take the boy and sleep at my mother-in-law's house in case I needed help during the night. I crept into her house, and everyone was already asleep. But I saw the baby's stomach was convulsing. I knew he would die.

"I woke up an aunt, and she held him while I knelt to pray. The spirit told me, 'If this child dies you should not cry.' So I told God, 'If you want this child, take him and put him in a good place.' Nyamweko died in my aunt's arms while I was praying.

"I was healed in 1984, and my son died in 1985. So you see, I have learned a lot from all I have experienced these past years. I am a Sunday school teacher and have been a women's group chair. I can read, and I like to read the Bible."

Rosa flashed us her wide innocent smile. She cradled sleepy Lucia in the worn kanga she wore to cover her own torn skirt.

"People say, 'So many people, even pastors, have begun well and then have fallen by the wayside.' I'm sure that won't happen to me! I just pray that until I leave this life God will keep me in his hands."

I knew it was unusual that this women's group had sent Rosa, such a young woman, to me. Usually middle-aged or older women were chosen. Although Rosa seemed unaware of it, the other women must have seen something unusual in her faith.

"I pray for the other women in my group, too" Rosa added, "so that their hearts will be turned to God. Some in the group are far behind in the ways of faith. Many are the same ones who had doubts about me. They still don't know enough about faith to know that God has spoken to me."

I smiled in response to her shy grin. And I thought, *Yes, Rosa, they know.*

5. Miriam—Making the Best of It

Miriam Achieng Odinga. Born 1949, Luo tribe, Musoma, Tanzania.

I met Miriam after the New Year's Day service in the town of Migori, on the western edge of Kenya. Her starched, white nurse's uniform and excellent use of English contributed to the impression that she was a competent woman. This large-boned, confident person could handle almost anything.

Bob, Chris, Lisen and I had been up late the night before, New Year's Eve. We sat in our dreary, cement-slab motel room, where the cold-water shower dripped steadily on the toilet seat.

All night we had listened to distant drums and African voices raised in traditional chant. It had brought a certain romance to our holiday here, evoking as it did all the romantic African movies we had ever seen, complete with drums reverberating out of a black night.

Only the next morning did we discover we had heard the Roho Israel church celebrating a New Year's service and not some tribal celebration. These were charismatic Christians who enjoyed bringing African flavor to their worship.

Because of the late night and because the rest of the family had departed in a flurry just that morning, I was battling a headache in the bright, morning glare.

Miriam had done some homework for her women's group before I arrived. She had collected the women's stories herself, writing them out in English. She gave me her own story, written in her own hand.

"I was born in 1949, May 30, at noon, when the sun is very hot, under a mango tree. Since I was born at noon, that's why I was called Achieng.

"My father, Daniel Opanga, was then working with the church in Musoma, Tanzania, as a pressman in the printshop, making the well-known hymnals *Tenzi za Rahoni.* He knew about God from his childhood, so I was brought up in a Christian home. I am the eighth child out of twelve children. Now only seven are alive.

"Every evening after meals, Father used to read us the Bible, mostly from the book of Proverbs. Through this book, I grew up respecting people older or younger, so I was also loved among the children.

"My mother, Susan Opanga, was a real mother of the family. She didn't like to see her children walking around to other houses, so she cooked things to satisfy us. She knew how to cook many things—cakes, bread, mendozzis. She even mended our clothes. Because of this, she was loved by all of us. Her grandchildren also liked to stay with her.

"Though Father earned little, he tried to educate us all. I attended school up to grade ten. After I joined the secondary school, I felt free. I followed what other girls were doing—and became pregnant. It was painful to both my parents to see me come back, but I needed to tell them the truth. My schooling stopped.

"After the delivery, my father tried again. He got me a chance in a teacher training college. I stayed there for one year. Then I decided to marry. The man I married had a wife already, which I discovered only after reaching his home. I ran away.

"I went to stay with my sister Loyce at Shirati. Here I had my second child. Some time later a woman came and asked to speak to me. She and her husband, Sospeter Odinga, had been married for many years and had never had children. She asked if I would agree to give her my two children and marry her husband. He was a Christian man who had experienced salvation.

"My sister Loyce and my parents approved of this plan, because they knew it was hard for a girl to find a man who could accept her two children. Everybody in the family was happy.

"After our marriage we had our first baby, Joyce Akinyi. When she was about to walk, polio paralyzed her. I can still remember how a missionary nurse at Shirati helped us. Joyce is still lame but can walk with crutches. She was lucky to get a chance in Joyland School for the Disabled in Kisumu. She's going to start her class six there.

"I have seven children, now. The firstborn will be in grade ten next year.

"Sospeter had worked at the mission hospital at Shirati for thirty-four years. But after he took a second wife, he lost his job there. I was lucky enough to be accepted in the nursing school, however. My husband returned to his homeland in Kenya. He found a job in a mission hospital there for two and a half years before they retired him. By this time I had finished school and joined him.

"We had many thoughts. How would we care for the children? How would we educate them when their father no longer had any income? But since he was a person who knew more about God, he was always satisfied and accepted any situation.

"I have the burden of caring for the whole family now. My income is all we have. But I'm happy; God helps me. I'm not saved [by this, Miriam seems to mean that she has not had a charismatic experience] but I know the Word of God. I have many verses to help me.

"I like going to church, and all my children like the Word of God. The two eldest are choir members. I pray that one day Jesus Christ will show me the right way. My husband also still loves God. He says that wives and children are the pleasures of this world. But he's sure that one day he'll be in the happy land, the promised land."

6. Hellen—I Couldn't Accept a Co-Wife

Hellen Ouko. Born 1943, Luo tribe, Kisumu, Kenya.

Hellen greeted us in her own living room wearing sneakers, a pretty dress, and an impish grin. Obviously her sugarcane crops and school teacher's salary had made her prosperous.

The obligatory doilies rested on the table and straight chairs. A few posters adorned the mud-plaster walls. Outside in the grass yard, she posed for a cheerful snapshot, surrounded by her tall, teenaged children. Then together we walked up a footpath to the local church, where we could talk without children listening.

"When my husband first started to hint about finding a second wife, I just couldn't believe it!" she confided to me. "We were Christians. We had promised each other we would be faithful and not take other partners. We had only been married four years and had a one-year-old daughter, Nelly.

"Our first child had been stillborn. For a year I didn't conceive again. That is a long time. I knew that relatives had been gossiping and urging Paul to find a hometown girl, one who would do better. But he had resisted their suggestions and took me to see a doctor instead.

"But several years later, when he first began hinting, I knew he was tempted. I thought about it all the time and grew thin. I knew I couldn't stand it if he brought a co-wife home.

"Gradually our love for each other lessened. I wanted to be a Christian, but I also went home to my mother repeatedly and begged her to let me stay.

" 'No,' she would tell me. 'You chose him and now you must stay with him.' Paul would come to get me, and my mother would send me off. Things would go better for a time, and then my husband would talk again about a second wife. I grew bitter.

"Though a son followed Nelly and then two more daughters, our relationship was on-again, off-again for ten years. We both grieved when our three-year-old girl died of malaria.

"Finally in 1974, I gave my permission for Paul to bring a second wife home. I was so tired of quarrels that I thought I didn't care anymore.

"I welcomed her politely at first. But when I saw Paul and this twenty-one-year-old girl honeymooning, I grew very angry. I felt neglected and jealous and spoke bitter words. The gap between us widened. Paul stopped supporting my family and seldom visited.

"I thought about two options—leaving him or committing suicide. In my tribe, the children belong to the husband. If I died or left, who would raise them? I was desperate.

"Finally I made a decision. I had been working for several years as a nursery school teacher. I would stay and support my children with my earnings and learn to depend on God alone.

"A last baby boy was born in 1975, into a family whose father seldom visited.

"I lived without a husband and raised my family alone for about ten years. It was very hard for me. Life was always a struggle as I tried to make decisions with no one to turn to but God.

"I had always been an active churchwoman. People thought I was strong and faithful. But in 1986, at a special convention, I was saved. I was convicted of my own sin, and a big change took place in my heart and my behavior. I had taken up smoking to help me relax and sleep. Now I stopped smoking and slept well.

"Before, when I preached to women's groups, I felt guilty. I knew I couldn't live up to my own words. Now I felt innocent; I could preach more freely.

"Eventually my husband saw the changes in me. Recently he once again began to support me and my four children, along with his younger wife and their seven children. Our relationship is better.

"If my daughters would find themselves in my situation, I would advise them to persevere—not desert their children. But I also want them to have enough education that they could support their own families if necessary.

"Polygamy is not easy for anyone. It brings quarrels and trouble. But it is a great temptation to men whose social status soars when they have more wives and children. I don't think a man can love two partners equally, so his life becomes unsteady and he moves away from Christ.

"I praise God for delivering me from bitterness. I have four healthy children, a fertile sugarcane *shamba*, and my job. I enjoy serving as secretary for my local congregation and for the regional women's group.

"I believe now that my twenty-three years of struggle were preparation for my salvation."

7. Zipporah—God Gave Me My Own Church

Zipporah Owango Agot. Born 1926, Luo tribe, Majiwa, Kenya.

Our little Fiat was loaded down with six passengers and luggage. The wheels sucked out of the viscous, red mud of the road ever more reluctantly as the holes deepened. The red clay was like glue, but Pastor Musa blithely waved us on. Majiwa village was still farther down the road.

In the sky, storm clouds threatened a downpour. Bob is an excellent driver, but we could all feel his tension as he pulled at the wheel and watched the sky. If it rained now, we would never be able to drive back out.

The countryside was beautiful, full of hills and little, green valleys. Charming, well-kept farms grew sugarcane, bananas, fruit, and maize. Finally our guide motioned, and we stopped beside an almost invisible footpath. We would go the rest of the way on foot to avoid getting the car stuck.

Bob and the children stayed with the car, issuing instructions: "Bring the woman out with you, and we'll drive back out before it rains and speak to her in the village instead."

We waded out of the car, sinking into the red goo. I took off my shoes and went barefoot. But the tall, dignified pastor did not stoop to this. Pregnant Rebecca also tried to pick her way through.

We walked a long time. I found myself enjoying the fresh, moist smells of growing things and the warm ooze between my toes. A woman traveled along the road toward us, chatting with her neighbor who carried a forty-pound load of bananas on her head. When she spied us she hurried over, shouting greetings to her old friend, Pastor Musa. She was about sixty, tough and agile, swinging her legs from the hip like an athlete. She chattered and laughed in a coarse voice that carried down the valley. She was Zipporah, a farmer and pastor. It was her shamba we were headed for.

The farm nestled in a valley among gentle hills. A small orchard of dwarf orange and lemon trees lined the clearing; beyond were immaculate fields. A county extension agent (or the African parallel) was there also waiting for Zipporah. Together they went off to inspect her crops.

At the edge of the clearing was a small mud-and-thatch hut. I knew it was Zipporah's church. She and another widow had built it themselves. They named it Majiwa, or "Strength."

We took pictures. We met Zipporah's sons, grandchildren, and assorted relatives who lived with her. We inspected the church. Only an hour later did we make our way back to the path and finally to the car. Bob was where I had left him; he apparently had not moved. He still watched the sky as if only his will could hold back the rain. Wedging our additional passenger into the Fiat, we gingerly turned back to run the gauntlet one more time through the red, gooey mud.

Once at the village market, Zipporah disappeared for a time. Then she motioned us to follow her to a tiny storeroom next to a shop, where we improvised tiny footstools to perch on. Her husband's brother owned the shop. He perched in the circle and added his own comments from time to time.

He was young and handsome, but with red-rimmed eyes. It took me awhile to realize that he was drunk. My anger flared as he offered some of his own opinions, such as "I know you Westerners are promiscuous, but we Africans don't like that. We don't like our women to live alone and act promiscuously. We are different from you!"

Zipporah cheerfully ignored this young brother-in-law and told us her story. She didn't spare the wrath she reserved for her former husband. In fact, it crossed my mind that while she was safely protected by the status of bringing her brother-in-law international guests, she wanted to set her record straight with his family once and for all.

She had been born, she told us, to a traditional family who brought their girls up to farm, grind, look after animals, and carry water and firewood. She never went to school. However, she married Amos Agot in the Anglican Church, and the young couple was nominally Christian. At age sixteen she bore the first of her seven living children: Elizabeth, Wilfred, James, Grace, Joyce, Bil, and Josphine.

To Zipporah's great disappointment, their life was full of quarrels and fights. Her husband beat her often, with little provocation. After about five years of this unhappy life, Zipporah divorced her husband and returned to her parents' home.

As I watched Zipporah and the sparks in her dark eyes, I could not imagine this feisty farmer allowing anyone to beat her. I wondered that she had lasted five years.

"While I was at home, I began attending an Anglican fellowship. It was here that I realized my sin," Zipporah said. "The Lord revealed to me that I was a jealous person, tough-headed and quick tempered. I received the Lord as my personal savior. Then I decided to go back to my former husband.

"My return was worse than I had feared. The beatings resumed. My husband did not like it that I was saved. He would not allow me to attend fellowship meetings with other Christians. I went anyway, knowing that when I went home I would be beaten or turned away with no place to sleep for the night.

"I was different now. I was able to hold my anger better. I no longer brewed pombe. And after a burial in the village, when the elders came to perform the traditional rituals, I refused to prepare food. I felt that my faith in Christ would not permit that.

"I trusted in the Lord. I remembered the Bible verse 'nothing can separate me from the love of God. . . .' And I thought, *I'll persevere. Someday I'll go to heaven.* I would hear about Stephen being stoned, and I was aware that I'd have to struggle too.

"Some time later, my husband began attending church services. He had a relationship with the Lord for six years. When I was around forty-two, however, the pressures of the world caught up with him. He married a second wife. Later he married two more wives. My life in that home became unbearable. My co-wives sided with our husband in his quarrels and fights. He refused completely to care for my immediate family unless I renounced and left the church.

"He had a job in town and later he moved there. I lived on the farm with the children. Somehow his money always disappeared in town. He paid for school fees and an occasional uniform for the children. I provided their food and clothes from my farm produce. His money went now for the families of my co-wives. I was angry. I was even more angry at his spending his pension money for more wives than I was about the beatings he had given me.

"I now attended a church that was beyond walking distance of my village. I often rode a matatu to church on Sunday. Finally another woman in my village, a widow, and I got together. We requested permission to build a small church in our own village. The church encouraged us in this and offered to come and help us build it.

"The villagers resented this project deeply, mostly because

they did not want a woman to found this church. The elders repeatedly warned me that they did not want my church. Traditionally, a woman cannot even put up a house without her husband's involvement, much less a church.

"Finally they called in my husband. Surprisingly, he changed his opposition and told the elders he was no longer opposed to my church. He could see nothing wrong with it! So what could the elders say? That is how, with God's guidance, our church was established.

"Still, to this day there is opposition. A teenage boy threatened to kill me just last week. Others have threatened things. Oh, I was afraid at first. But with prayer I gathered my courage. We built the church, and now about ten people worship there each Sunday. It gives me great comfort.

"There is peace in my house now even though my husband refuses to visit us. The Lord has showered blessings on me. I have a good farm, good children. I just pray that God will guide my daughters to good husbands. You can't tell how people will turn in the future. Me? Well, I can't say I'm happy. I would be happier if my husband came back."

8. From the Serengeti Plain to Levirate Marriage

Chris and I sat on the flat top of a battered Land Rover as it lurched along a deserted track in the Serengeti National Park. We wore windbreakers against the dew and morning chill, but the tropical sun was hot on my hair and face, melting all the tight muscles. I smelled the hood-high, golden, sun-dried grasses with delight. I didn't care that they would camouflage the lions from our sight. The great soaring birds, whether buzzards or hawks, wheeled into blue skies before us; smaller jeweled songbirds, blue, green and gold, darted into thorn trees.

I have never seen a clean sky before, I thought. *I have never smelled clean air.* It was the smell and the sun that was so luxurious. And the pollen, the sweetness of dry grass, top-heavy with seed. It is illegal to ride unprotected like this in a game park, of course. But we came into the park through the back gate and there was no one to protest. No tourists, no park guards, no one at all for another fifty miles or so.

The action all centered on the east. There tourists arrived past Mount Kilimanjaro, passed the Ngorongoro Crater, and circled into the Serengeti where they slept in one of the beautiful lodges. They were carefully protected inside tourist vans painted with zebra stripes and told to keep their hands inside the windows please. No matter how magnificent the animals you saw, there was still that sense of containment. The zoo walls were merely reversed.

Besides, the big annual migration of the one and a half million wildebeest was over. They were far to the north, looking for green grass. Much of the game, including predators and birds, went with them. So the park was quiet.

Inside the Land Rover, Jan and Peter Shetler, community development workers, were driving. They looked with veteran eyes for game, paid attention to directions, and fed their two preschool sons. They were the ones who boiled our water, packed provisions, checked the spare tires, and promised us a foray into their favorite spot in Tanzania.

Bob was busy watching for signs of tsetse flies up close and lions from afar. The children were tired and hot and conducting a fight that was just subtle enough to keep them from getting yelled at. Ludia Mbeba, a gracious, lady-like Tanzanian who was able to enjoy herself anywhere, offered to come along on this trip to help translate and conduct interviews. This was her second trip to a game park.

It was tight and claustrophobic inside the van. We were all tired of the lurching, of the terrible dirt tracks and ruts. When Pete suggested riding on top, we were eager to take turns.

Chris and I smiled at each other and drew long, relaxed breaths. This was the Africa I had imagined—wild, free, unpopulated. We saw a long string of elephants, like a frieze up ahead, tiny cut-out silhouettes. Chris and I felt the Land Rover veer off the track into the field. We bumped around miniature thorn trees and rotten logs and drew closer.

The elephants were easily spooked, which meant they were probably being poached. They trotted ahead of us at a good clip. Suddenly the guard elephant, the last one, turned around and headed for our van. She fanned her ears, feinted, then returned.

But our van didn't disappear. It crawled along, keeping up with the disgruntled elephants in the distance. The guard elephant tried again. This time a long trumpet erupted behind her flagged ears; she made a surprisingly agile about-face lunge toward us.

For the first time it dawned on me that elephants are indeed quite fast. At the pace this one was moving, it would be upon us soon. *I am a mother with responsibilities,* I thought *What am I doing here in the open with absolutely nothing between myself and a charging angry elephant!*

In no time, without even an exchanged glance, Chris and I were scrambled off our perch. The safe inhabitants inside yelled through our legs, which blocked their windshield view, "Stay where you are! Stay! We're moving!"

The van was already moving, turning in the opposite direction, toward scrub trees and treacherous, camouflaged, little drainage ditches. *Be careful, Pete!* I prayed, imagining a tire bursting on a thorn branch or an axle breaking.

As soon as the elephant saw our intentions she gave a satisfied snort. She went back to her follow-up position in line, her duties successful. Chris and I hung on and trembled. Our limbs were weak, yet we felt oddly triumphant.

Along the river the trees formed green clusters. Closer to us were the grazing gazelles, kudzu, a few zebras—peaceful in the golden fields. The rivers always looked dangerous here. Brown, opaque. Home of crocodiles, hippos, bacteria, hidden things.

This is the real Africa, I thought, *the extravagant beauty always sharpened by hidden dangers—the running lion, the scorpion, the snake.* No wonder Africans were not individualists. They walked through life into the afterlife, accompanied by great numbers of family, relatives and clan members, and were greeted by the same on the other side. There was safety in numbers, in the familiar.

The tie with a husband or a wife was a weak one. Who could depend on one other person for safety or happiness? How much laughter could only two voices create? So one married the whole clan of the mate, annexing a whole group of relatives. They provided a circle of protection around one's children, the many, many children one longed to have.

Nothing hung on one person alone. There was no hero-worship. The strength was in the forged links between each person in the group. These members did not try to shake themselves free, rise above the group, form an alternate identity. Because out there lurked imminent danger.

Most of the women I talked to had never seen an elephant, had never visited the game park. How could they? It was so far into the park that one had to sleep overnight, and the only accommodations there were for tourists, at a month's wages per night.

But they had stories of lone rampaging wildcats, or lions mauling children or snakes dropping from the ceiling and slithering off again. The terrors of nature were all too real: a healthy child drooping with fever one evening and dead the next day, a long drought, hunger, and old people dying from weakness. None of them had ever seen public television specials on the charms of wildlife. They had no romantic notions about conservation. Nature for them was an adversary, highly respected, but dangerous. For women who had to wade into crocodile-infested water with bare legs each day to fetch water, there was only the alertness of fear, and the security of being one of a group poised to help each other.

The farther away from the big towns we went, the more remote the villages, the more I saw that the old social structures—including polygamy and inheritance marriages—were a hedge of protection. They provided security within the clans against a frightening and hostile environment.

On the Serengeti and in the remote villages of Tanzania, women did not embroider their existence with romance, as did the women of the Western world. Strong, laughing and singing as they walked to the river and to the field to work, they were obviously finding happiness in life without romance.

When they agreed to the husband chosen for them, they did not expect him to be fun, a companion, a kindred spirit. He would simply be a husband, with all the authority and, if hopes were realized, protection, that implied.

If he died, and the clan provided a substitute, well, that husband too would offer protection. The woman would not call him by name—that would seem too familiar. But she would call him husband and honor the conventions. She would give him certain rights and privileges in exchange for his protection and that of his clan.

The practice of providing a relative to substitute for a recently dead husband is called levirate marriage. It is described in Deuteronomy 25:5-10 and was practiced by the Jews well up into New Testament times.

> If brothers dwell together, and one of them dies and has no son, the wife of the dead shall not be married outside the family to a stranger; her husband's brother shall go in to her, and take her as his wife, and perform the duty of a husband's brother to her. And the first son whom she bears shall succeed to the name of his brother who is dead, that his name may not be blotted out of Israel.

This practice solved a lot of problems for the woman, who did not stand to inherit anything upon her husband's death. If she had no sons, the home, fields, food, and belongings reverted to her husband's brothers and family. She was left homeless and penniless.

If she wanted to leave, perhaps to marry a "stranger," then her children might have to stay behind with her late husband's family. The most loving thing a clan could do was to offer her a permanent place with them through the authority of a new husband. Sometimes the coupling took place as part of the funeral ceremony. The children produced this way were understood to belong to the dead husband's name.

Some levirate marriages were authentic unions, such as ones described in the following section by Philomena and Dorika. Dorika, however, described the social pressure on her new husband by those who claimed that the children were not really his and that he needed his own wife as well.

Prisca told us what it felt like to be the first wife who was asked to accept a levirate marriage that eventually broke up her own.

If a woman were past childbearing years, however, or if no appropriate or willing relative were found, then the widow might not be offered such a solution. Her problems were multiplied. Particularly if she had no sons, her old age would be insecure indeed. She would have to farm and make her own way or accept handouts from relatives, living on the edges of their compounds. That was the plight of Plista, who was alone, poor, and fearful of the future.

And beyond marriage, what else would there be for the African woman? Well, there would be work, always hard work, work to give meaning to life. In her work she would be able to control her world, feed her children, feel her power. There would be friends, jokes, singing, and all that love for the children at her breast.

And in old age, if she were lucky, she would sit back, under her son's protection. She would soak in all her sons' respect and love. She would survive all right without all the Western fuss about romance.

9. Philomena—A Dead Husband, A New Baby

Philomena Odeny. Born 1952, Luo tribe, Musoma, Tanzania, Gogo, Kenya.

Philomena was not pretty, but she more than compensated for that. She had a typical Luo build, tall, thin, long-boned, graceful, with high cheekbones. But her teeth were an orthodontic nightmare, long and splayed apart. Still, bad teeth do not stop a woman from working hard or producing babies. Her dead husband's uncles would have been happy to have her. No, it was

Philomena's own fault that she had gone unmarried over a year after Odeny had died.

Our whole family sat at her table, along with the local pastor and his daughter, Rebecca Osiro, who had joined me in this project. Chris and Lisen had been summoned from their car-watching job to join us for a huge and delicious dinner, which they wolfed down. Chicken and sauce, boiled greens and, instead of the expected ugali, cooked bananas—a wonderful treat.

The small, African-village house was immaculate. It had been freshly smeared in a two-tone pattern with ocher and tan mud washes. The courtyard was freshly swept, with broom patterns carefully dragged in the dust. The round toddler perched on Philomena's thin arm was happy and well fed. Obviously Philomena was a good mother and manager.

Her village of a half dozen houses nestled in fields of sugarcane, bananas, and maize, the green stalks as high as our heads. We parked on a dirt road, then walked in from the road along a footpath worn hard from the traffic of bare feet. It skirted the fields for a kilometer or so.

Here in Western Kenya was a delightful green farmer's belt, noted for its large sugar cane plantations. But in these tiny, farming villages scattered among the plantations, life was still traditional, as we were about to find out.

We sat at the bare wood table and listened to Philomena's story. A Catholic girl, she had married Odeny in Tanzania. She had then been baptized in the Protestant church where he was an active elder. At age sixteen she gave birth to a son. Bernard was followed by Erastus, Rosemary, and Teressa. They had a happy life together and seldom quarreled. While Odeny went to Bible school, Philomena took a six-month domestic science course.

When her husband's father died, they followed tradition and returned to his Kenyan village to live. There the Kenya church invited Odeny to continue his leadership and assigned him a church to care for. The church was far enough away that Odeny often set out on Saturday and returned Sunday after he had preached. It was hard work for him, traveling so much. Eventually the church arranged to give Odeny a house there and began to fix it up for him. Odeny eagerly began to plant a field there on weekends.

During this time Odeny, Philomena, and the four children did not build their own house on the family homestead as tradition would have dictated. It was always important for a son to build his own house, no matter how small, in his father's village. This symbolized his place in the clan structure. But Odeny was too busy preparing for his family's move.

About this time, Odeny began to feel pain in his legs and stomach. He became more and more ill. Doctors finally told him that he had cancer. He spent one week in the hospital; he came home deathly sick in a *matatu*, the crowded van which buses village people from place to place. Later he had to go back to the hospital.

Philomena was nine months pregnant with her fifth child. It was hard for her to make the trip to the hospital. She dreamed that Odeny had passed away, and the children were mourning him. Again she dreamed, and in the dream saw a Bible reference, 1 Timothy 6:12: "Fight the good fight of the faith; take hold of the eternal life to which you were called when you made the good confession in the presence of many witnesses."

That verse comforted her the next day as she went to the hospital and watched Odeny suffer. At nine o'clock in the evening he died. "I felt strong. I didn't feel the grief at first," Philomena marveled. She went into labor several hours later, and at 9:00 a.m. her fifth child, a son, was born. He was named Charles Okun Odeny, after his father.

Philomena, her new baby, and her dead husband all came home from the hospital on the same day. The traditional tribal elders were full of consternation. Many vague fears had been stirred by the bizarre train of events that had occurred. The old men conferred about burial and purification ceremonies.

They decided that Philomena was no longer welcome in their huts. Everyone knew that the evil spirits which cause death hover around the remaining loved ones. The bereaved usually stayed close to their own houses to avoid harming anyone else.

But Philomena didn't have her own house. The clan quickly cleaned out an old hut which was no longer used. Its roof was caving in, and there were holes in the walls. Here they brought a pallet for Philomena and her new baby to rest on, and here they brought the dead Odeny and laid his body to await burial.

She was told not to wander around the village until the death rituals were over. If she entered any hut in the village the head of the house might die. She was not supposed to shake hands with men when greeting them or give her baby to anyone to hold but the old village women. She was told that several elderly uncles of her husband would be willing to marry her immediately. (In some cases one of the death rituals involved coupling the widow with her husband's uncle.)

Other common practices included forbidding the widow to wash or comb her hair. Her clothes were torn. She was to wail and cry continuously.

"If a wife dies, does a husband mourn and cry?" I once asked a young man interpreter.

"No," he said, puzzled at my question.

If the real tears ran dry, the widow rubbed red pepper in her eyes. Sometimes she was even beaten. During the funeral, visitors sometimes rampaged through her fields and garden, eating and taking everything. She would expect her husband's relatives to claim most of the family belongings. In some vague sense, the wife was felt to be partly at fault for her husband's death.

As Philomena lay in a weakened condition in the dilapidated hut with her dead husband, the reality of his death hit her at last. She felt deep grief. She was partly comforted by the tiny life beside her, born hours after Odeny's death and bearing his name. God had taken her husband and given her this baby. She decided to trust God in all this. She would refuse a marriage she was certainly not ready for, despite pressure from her in-laws. She would act as courageously as she could.

The Christians rallied to help Philomena. They decided to begin building her a house of her own. On the day of the burial, they pitched in and cut the poles. The relatives would also have liked to help but hesitated. Beginning the foundation of a new house was something only a husband did. Whoever did that work would be known henceforth as Philomena's husband, the elders said.

The first persons to relate to an unclean person were also susceptible to bad omens. They used to make the captives take on those chores in the old days to protect themselves from risk. So the people were afraid. But the Christians showed no fear of Philomena and comforted her. They gave Odeny a church burial and worked hard on her house with no grave consequences to anyone.

Philomena gathered her strength and moved to her own house. Sometimes she visited her husband's elderly uncle's house. But she refrained from visiting others or shaking hands. She gave the baby freely to others to hold, however, and ignored some of the other purification practices. People watched her and after three months had gone by, admitted that no misfortunes seemed to have fallen on her.

"People usually don't like to admit when they are wrong," Philomena sighed, "but a few now accepted me. Others went to the witchdoctor to protect themselves against me. I decided that God is the giver and creator of everything, and I could trust him to take care of us. I would stick to my words and follow God's way. I knew that nothing bad would befall me."

As the months went by, the clan began to discuss Philomena's future. A woman does not live alone in an African village without some man's protection. Traditionally, the dead husband's younger brother is a good prospect for a levirate marriage. The children produced from this union belong to the dead man, and the whole family continues their concern and care for the children as before. If a woman finds another man and leaves the village, her children usually stay behind to be raised by the family.

"We want you to raise your own children," they told her. "You are a good mother." They suggested Lukas Mbai Odeny, her brother-in-law, as a husband.

Lukas was a good man and unmarried, though younger than Philomena. He was a Christian too, and for him there would be some hard choices. If he took Philomena, most people would say that she and the children really belonged to his brother. He would have scant respect unless he married his own wife later.

Nevertheless, he let her know that he wanted to have a marriage ceremony (not normal practice for an inheritance marriage). He would pay a bride-price for her and consider her his own wife.

Philomena was happy. The thought of marrying another man and abandoning her children or of accepting a man who did not care much about them was unthinkable. Lukas would be a close relative to the children and would care for them and her. One year and eight months after she became a widow, Philomena married again. She has since given birth to a little girl, Rael.

"God calls me now," she said, "to tell others who are in sorrow, who stick to the traditional ways, that there is nothing to fear. Bad things will not happen to them. That is the message God has given me to teach to others. We do not need to live in fear of evil spirits or omens. God is always with us."

Many Christians continue to pray for this couple. They know that the pressure on Lukas to take another wife will be enormous. But for now, the Spirit is present in their marriage and family.

"Jesus' love for mankind washes away all the sin in the world," said Philomena. "I thank the Lord that when the right time came, he gave me a Christian and loving husband."

10. Dorika—A Levirate Marriage of Love

Dorika Nginina. Born 1937, Mluri tribe, Ruwanga, Kenya.

"I married at thirteen but it took me ten years to have a child! I was the only wife, and my husband was kind. He took me to a hospital to see what was wrong. After that I had four children. The smallest one was still nursing when my husband died."

Dorika was filled with energy and spoke with animation. I marvelled at her solid, energy-filled body and extroverted personality as she waved her hands and smiled.

"After his death in 1971, I saw many things about my own life that were not right. I had been attending church, but now I really began following Jesus. Other people said, 'She's so fervent, she'll forget it all soon.' But they were wrong. I've been growing every day since then.

"When I was left with four children, I thought it was better to remarry within the family than to go outside. So I followed custom and married my husband's uncle very soon afterwards. We loved each other, and he didn't have another wife. So he wasn't forced to marry me, although it was arranged by the clan. He paid a bride-price for me so our children would be his. I was thirty-four years old, and he was younger. We went to catechism together. We were baptized two years later.

"Together we had three children. In 1973 and 1974 I lost two boys, ages six and four, from my first husband. That was very hard for me. They got sick and died.

"People laughed at my husband and said, 'Dorika is not really your wife. You inherited her. Why don't you get your own wife?'

"So he married another wife. I thought, *If he is leaving God, I will go on myself. I won't abandon my faith.* But he says he still is close to Jesus. He can't take communion now, but I believe, too, that he is still a Christian. He still has faith.

"I like his second wife. She's a young child. I take care of her. She was from another denomination, but I counseled her to go into the church of her husband. So she goes to our church now. They welcome her there. They are waiting to see her spirit before her baptism. She needs to repent of her polygamous marriage, but our church doesn't ask her to leave her husband.

"Four years ago I was appointed an elder in our church. It is my responsibility to visit if I see someone backsliding. I am to visit the sick and dying, to give comfort. I enjoy this work. We pray together, and I counsel them, help them. This past week I visited a woman who had left the church completely but is now coming back."

Dorika laughed, and went on talking, "It is easy for me to talk to people and advise them. They like me. They often listen to me. I suppose that is my talent.

"My life is very full. I now have eight grandchildren. My son's family lives with me while he is away doing government work. His wife came to help me farm, to plant. I care for her children and for two others born to my son with another girl. Even if one hasn't paid the bride-price, the father's family often can claim the children."

Dorika's eyes seemed to be clouded with cataracts although she was only fifty years old. She said, "I can't see well, so I ask the children to get the Bible and hymnbook out after supper each night. They read to me.

"I especially like to hear Ephesians 2:4 when I think about the deaths of my two children. 'But God, who is rich in mercy, out of the great love with which he loved us, even when we were dead through our trespasses, made us alive together with Christ by grace you have been saved.'

"I don't ask God to take away my problems. I ask him to give me faith and love. I pray that God will go on with me throughout my life. I remember what life used to be like. When I was young, I made liquor. Everyone comes to your house then and drinks, touches each other. It's not a clean way of living. Now with Jesus I am much freer. I can talk to a man and no one fears. They know I'm honest.

"I make sure the children get to Sunday school and learn about God. Otherwise, if children are not in the habit of going to worship, they will soon be lost. If I see people are sinning I go to them and I say, 'You're a grown person, you have intelligence. Why are you doing these things? Why waste your life?' "

Dorika prepared to go. She had walked a long distance to see us at her pastor's house, but she seemed as vivacious as ever. There was always field work waiting to be done and the children to cook for.

11. Prisca—My Heart Was Broken

Prisca Tason. Born 1924, Luo tribe, Kowak, Tanzania, Shirati, Tanzania.

Prisca's face was black and strongly chiseled. She was handsome and impressive, and her large frame was strong. She bore fourteen children over a thirty-year period and twelve are still living. It is an impressive record, even in Tanzania. In her sixties, she was still active, earning her own living. She walked down to Lake Victoria and bought fish. This she carried back and barbecued in the market over charcoal to sell to those who came to visit people in the hospital. While she waited for customers, she crocheted baby sweaters to sell as well. Prisca was a businesswoman.

As she told me her story she went to great pains to have me understand that her Christian marriage of thirty years was destroyed by a levirate marriage suggested to her husband by his family. They asked him to marry his brother's young widow, and he was happy to do it. Without consulting his wife and twelve children, he brought another woman into the house. They all lived together for eight years.

"I was very angry about it. Later I was able to ask God to forgive me, but not at first. I felt a lot of doubt and turmoil. My heart was broken. I couldn't think straight. Yet I couldn't talk about it to others. Any help I got came straight from God. Aside from God I was completely alone in my grief.

"Sometimes, when I felt most alone, the children would come and help me, and say, 'Mama, you know who you can go to!'

"Two more children were born to me during those years, but now there were no longer the financial resources. My husband began to provide more for his younger wife and her baby and less for us. Those last two children eventually died. I began to feel like a poor relative in the house."

Prisca's grief over this rather common family event came from her strong Christian goals for her family. When she was young, she managed to go to a local girls' school for one year. Her family was resistant to this anyway. But when the school began to teach the girls that they should not work in their gardens on Sunday, that was the last straw. They took her home.

Then she arranged to have a teacher visit her. She did a self-study program at home for two years. At age eighteen she ran away from home and went to school at Shirati.

"I wanted to be a person of God, that's why I wanted school so badly," she remembered. After she had learned to read, she was baptized in Shirati.

She returned home and there met Tason Tiengo, a Christian. Because he did not have money for her bride-price, they eloped. They notified their bishop, Elam Stauffer, however. He gave strict instructions to Tason that they should live separately until he had arranged things with the families. This he did, even obtaining Prisca's parents' permission for Tiengo to pay them as he could. The young couple had a proper church wedding after that, which was a relief to them both.

Over the years they built a strong family and remained in the church. It was not until tribal custom entered the picture that trouble began. With the new combined family, no one felt at peace any longer. Finally, in 1972, Tiengo and his second wife moved away. This left Prisca to raise her twelve children alone.

There was great distance now between Tiengo and his children. He no longer helped them. When his son wanted to get married, it would have been customary for his father to provide cows for a bride-price. Tiengo was unwilling.

"He had to buy his own cows." Prisca sighed as though this was something shameful indeed. This first son went to America to school and now works for Radio Tanzania. He is paying school fees for three siblings still in school. The other children don't remember their father well.

"When I was so angry at my husband, I tried to discipline myself. Whenever I thought of him, I went to Jesus and prayed. What Tiengo did was wrong because he was a Christian. It brought difficulties for all of us. I believe Satan took hold of his heart.

"After I was able to accept his loss, I saw that Jesus could take the place of a husband in my life. Jesus is now my husband. Jesus has given me joy! I decided a long time ago not to remarry, but to live alone and make a good life for myself.

"If my husband comes to visit, now I am able to welcome him, cook for him. If he dies, I will let him be buried here as my husband. And if he would come back, I would accept him—not in a conjugal way, but in name. I welcome him in Jesus' name. I try to help the children forgive him as well. All of my children are Christians, and that is one of my great joys."

12. Plista—Where Will I Be in the Morning?

Plista Oyugi. Born 1941, Luo tribe, Kanyamkago, Tanzania, Ogwedhi-Sigawa, Kenya.

We came to know Plista by accident. We had set out that morning from a town in the southwestern corner of Kenya with an interpreter, our family, and a driver in a rented, four-wheel-drive truck. We climbed rocky hills along an almost impassible track. This land was dry, used by Maasai for grazing large herds of skinny, wild-horned cattle. It was sparsely populated.

We arrived, hot, dusty, and exhausted from the truck's jouncing at the mission settlement where we were expected. Vera Hanson came out of the house frowning. "You weren't supposed to come today. Didn't you get our message in town? The Maasai all left for the far hills for a circumcision ceremony!"

Several hours later, after Vera and her housekeeper Plista had put together a simple but delicious meal for us and our crushed spirits had revived, I remembered Rebecca Njau's advice to me as a story-collector: "There is always someone to talk to. Look around!"

Plista sat down with me graciously. She was a large, matriarchal, very black woman with a dignified manner and a kind face. Her upper teeth were separated in front (a local sign of beauty), and six of her front teeth on the bottom were missing according to custom.

We joked about that at first. "Oh," she said, "children used to be susceptible to lockjaw. We believe that is where the Luo custom began. We always removed the six teeth, and then we could feed a person through a straw if we had to. It was a sign of growing up. I longed to have it done.

"Then people couldn't tease me and say, 'See, you still have your baby teeth.' But that is a custom we don't practice anymore."

As I asked Plista to tell me about herself, it became apparent this woman had experienced hardship throughout her life.

Simply, without self-consciousness, she drew me a brief picture. She seemed surprised at my interest.

I discovered that here was a woman widowed in her forties, still vigorous but owning nothing. She had no security for her old age, no place in a secure family or clan, no protection. In her case, both of the traditional safety nets—a son to inherit his father's place in the clan or a levirate marriage to another member of the clan—were missing.

"I seemed to have bad luck, even before I was born. When my mother was in labor with me, lightning struck her house and it burned. My father was away in Tanzania, looking for land. She couldn't drag her misfortune into someone else's house. [Custom forbids someone who has had misfortune to sleep in another's house, for fear they will bring the evil spirits along with them.]

"So in the pouring rain, she built a small shelter and spent the night there. In the morning I was born. My mother was unconscious, very ill. She couldn't breastfeed me, so neighbors got some sheep's milk for me.

"When I was four my mother died. I was left to live with my father and two brothers. While I was still very young, I was taught to cook and carry water. I was overworked beyond my age.

"Because it was not a good home situation, I got married young. My husband was a good man, but we too had misfortune. Four children were born to us, three girls and one boy. Two girls and the son died, leaving only my one daughter. I didn't conceive more children for many years. Finally, in 1976, a fifth child was born, but it died during a Caesarean section birth. My husband took a second wife.

"We had been living in Tanzania where my husband had a job. But after he lost the job, we returned here to Ogwedhi, to his father's home. My husband suffered with a long illness and died in 1982.

"The younger wife had a boy and a girl. She was still bearing children. She was taken by my husband's younger brother. But I was alone. For two years I continued to live and farm on the land. But finally the family ran me off. I had no son to inherit, and the clan wanted to sell the land. The chief had allotted some household goods to me when my husband died. This had annoyed them.

"I had been happy with my husband. He loved me. It was a good marriage. I think now that some of the relatives were jealous. They thought I had taken him over too much. Now they talk through other people, use threatening words about me. Sometimes I even fear they could murder me. So I put my life in God's hands and don't fight back.

"No, I would never go to court to claim the house or land to farm," she said in answer to my question. "People here practice witchcraft. I might lose my life in such a battle."

Plista's life had changed in many ways. When the clan failed to help her, the local church gave her physical and spiritual support. "Nobody else cared about me," she said.

She began to attend faithfully and later took it on herself to clean the church. Eventually she was appointed to be one of the church committee members. "I visit the sick and pray with them, and I encourage those whose faith is weak. I am expected to visit those who sin. You need to be a devoted Christian to do this. People welcome me when I visit, all except my husband's family—they don't receive me well.

"I was offered this job to help the Hansons here at the mission, so the Christian community was concerned about me. I rent a small, thatched house in the village.

"But you see, I am always worried. I own no house, no land. I have nothing to farm on, no place to plant crops for myself. I think, *Where will I be in the future, when I am old*? Every sunset I look up and think, *Where will I be in the morning? When will I be chased away again?*

"I love my daughter, but she cannot help me. In fact, I am helping her. Her husband also died, and she has seven children and is very poor. She lived with me for several months, and I am raising my eldest grandchild.

"I mourn sometimes for my husband, for the children. I wish that I had a son, a son to stand up for me. But my son's death was a natural thing. I have accepted it, not like the misfortune of my relatives hating me.

"When I really feel troubled, I go to my Pastor and I ask him to read from the Bible. Job is the most helpful biblical passage—it comforts me."

CHAPTER

The Refugees

1. Mombasa, Kenya

While I left for a month in Zaire to interview women there, traveling by bush plane and Land Rovers, Bob and the children baby-sat a lovely mansion. It was set in marvelous gardens in the English highlands, a thirty-minute drive outside Nairobi. It was available for only two months while the owners were away. They appreciated having someone living in it, so they rented it at an absurdly low figure.

When we moved in, the English farm manager accompanied by two large dogs, showed us around. He taught us to work the locks fastening the doors. The front door had a huge, removable, wooden barricade. Metal grillwork doors locked off the bedrooms. We were to lock all inner doors when we went to bed. The dogs slept outside the bedroom.

There was an electronic burglar alarm to summon the private guard company whose van patrolled the road, and there were manual airhorns by the bed to blow in case we got in trouble. We were warned to keep track of our food supplies because the cook was prone to steal food. A Maasai-looking young fellow guarded the house at night. He wore a skirt and carried a spear as he patrolled inside the locked fence.

In the yard, orchid-like succulents bloomed in the crotches of huge old trees. Exotic tropical plants flowered in profusion, covering the iron fence and gate with green. The ibis swooped in on huge wings for water, dipping over red and white calla lilies, and smaller birds sang with the dawn. It was paradise.

Although we tried to forget those locks and fences, it remained apparent that we were the prisoners, looking out from our wealth at a hostile countryside. There the country people walking on the road did not smile at us as they had in other towns and villages. There was only suspicion.

It was Mau Mau country, where the bitter rebellion against the English usurpers of the country's best plantation land took place twenty years ago. The landed English still gathered at a local country club to play bowls. They chatted about the old days, when the Africans had shown respect and addressed them as "Bwana" and "Madame."

Whites were outsiders. We were allowed to stay because of our property and our money. But it was obvious none of it really belonged to us. The local Africans watched and waited, knowing that the highlands had always been theirs—and should be again. Meanwhile they picked tea and farmed for white employers. They stole what they could and did not show up when they felt like drinking instead.

The whites were rich refugees, making their uneasy and usually impermanent homes on the rich, fertile land laced with streams and old trees. Their fine English houses with French doors opened to gardens and a vista of hilly tea plantation beyond. Yet the doors would always have metalwork traceries to keep out the anger, murder, thievery, and despair of their black neighbors.

I hated to say good-bye to my family. I felt in some vague way that this living environment was the most foreign of all. I felt that I should stay and protect them from the hostile vibrations I felt there.

Yet the highlands are so beautiful, the air so absolutely clean and crisp, and the clouds so white and high, that one could forget. The sun shining full on that sharp yellow-green of the tea, bouncing off again in gold shafts, and the brown-and-white cows grazing made forgetting easy.

Karen (Isak Dinesen) Blixen had lived on just such a place, in the Ngong Hills outside Nairobi. I reminded myself that settlers like her had worked hard. They had braved many dangers, like black-water fever and malaria. Many had failed. Others had brought education and hospitals. History was complex. And the villains were no worse than the American settlers who chased

Indians away so that they might produce something out of nature's profligate ways. Yet the pain remained, on both sides of the iron fences.

When I returned from Zaire, it was soon time to leave the mansion. It was almost Christmas. Once again we packed all we owned into our little Fiat and went on the road. We had some visits to make in various parts of Kenya but planned to make our way to the coast. When Christmas came and we were all homesick, we would be staying in Mombasa, that delightful Arab town that has welcomed sailors and traders to African shores since the time of Christ.

Down out of the cool, green hills, terraced with well-kept Kikuyu farms and the large plantations, we dropped. Finally we came to flat, low, scrub country, where the heat rose in dry, shimmering waves, and there was no water. Here huge, open spaces, home of scrub bush and tsetse flies, led past the Amboseli and Tsavo national parks. It was country suited to lions, not people.

As we got closer to the coast, tall, bare-branched baobab trees dotted the fields like living monuments to God, each one of such singular shape and character that we kept stopping to photograph them. Hot and dusty, we covered the 450 kilometers as quickly as we could. We cheered when we finally saw glimpses of the Indian Ocean and traffic signs indicating an approaching city.

The only place we found to rent during this prime Christmas tourist season was a cold-water, one-room flat where we cooked on a hot-plate. It huddled in the shadow of several famous tourist hotels on the beach. It provided fun the big hotels wouldn't have—we had real garbage cans in the back and little monkeys raided them continually, babies clutching their mother's bellies. We made sure to keep our doors closed to the curious, sharp-teethed little thieves but we laughed at their antics.

We enjoyed hiking down the beach to a less densely populated spot. There we walked out on the sand bars, a quarter mile or so through the 105-degree, clear, blue Indian Ocean, to where a mild surf broke on the coral reefs. We swam only in the morning and evening, after the full sun had diminished; kept our shirts on as protection from the sizzling tropic sun. Mombasa is hot! Bob, who had had a touch of skin cancer on his forehead the year before, kept out of the sun, enjoying the evening beach instead.

Lisen and I headed out one late afternoon when there was no one else in sight. The sun had dropped and the sky was flat as I lay on my back in a foot of buoyant, warm seawater. Lisen practiced snorkeling nearby. Gradually my seething mind slowed down to the present. Green seagrass floated in the clear, blue water, and I held smooth tiny white shells in my hand like a rosary.

Gradually long, lilac clouds in horizontal layers formed on the horizon. In fifteen minutes they had floated across the sky, over my head. The westerly sun began to glint gold on the palms, and the shore figures became silhouettes. The wind cooled, and Lisen and I stayed submerged in the warm water up to our necks, reluctant to move.

Lisen always begged to carry home everything she could find. I had learned to limit her to three treasures each trip. She agonized over which three treasures to keep. We were happy as we ran over the sharp coral rocks, climbed the sand hill, and headed home in the twilight.

The Indian Ocean was friendly there, boasting nothing more than occasional patches of black, spiny sea urchins. But there was plenty more for the adventurous. On our shore, the ocean had worn away deep holes in the coral rock. At high tide, these fifteen-foot-deep aquariums filled with fresh salt water and amazing creatures which low tide stranded there.

Many beginners used these holes to practice their snorkeling; it seemed safer than the whole ocean. These holes boasted everything—the inquisitive little zebra fish, angelfish, coral gardens, tiny octopuses and eels. Both Chris and Lisen could snorkel well and showed little fear, although Lisen was by nature more cautious.

One day she surfaced and said, "Mommy, there's a snake down there." Reassuring her that it was probably an eel, I dived in myself. As I floated on the sunny surface of the pool, each darting fish and creature was clearly visible.

Below, on the rough coral floor, was a large, coiled snake. It was watching me with interest, although it seemed contented. I left in a hurry, heart pounding, telling myself and the children that what we had seen was impossible. I had never heard of a snake that lived in salt water. Our landlord assured us he never had either.

Later I learned from a book about tropical marine life that there was a sea snake, highly poisonous, that lived in tropical waters. Although we never saw the snake again, we grew more cautious. I warned the children about touching strange-looking coral and protrusions that often turned out to be weird but harmless forms of life, like sea cucumbers, sandworms, and anemones.

Chris, our adventurer, who snorkeled with friends far out in the surf, taught us about the stings of scorpion fish and stonefish, but he also taught us to see the magnificent beauty in the colors of coral, the bizarre fish, the shells, and the underwater grasses.

Like all life in the wild, the ocean's extravagant beauty was laced with a trace of danger lurking in the corners, in the unseen. How differently this shaped the beliefs and culture of people who lived with "nature created," instead of "nature subdued." They combined risk and fear with a deep understanding of their place in this world.

We were surrounded on that holiday by German tourists who stayed in the big hotels. Strains of their oompah bands followed us even on the sand. The Africans who waded along the beaches carrying Maasai spears, shields, beads and other mementos had learned how to sell in German.

We learned that Europeans generally wore skimpier swim suits than we were used to, even though most of them were past middle age. Some women swam topless. The stout, old men wore G-string briefs. No one seemed embarrassed by sagging, white flesh. We saw that our American fetish for perfect bodies was not shared. The athletic, lean, brown bodies of Africans seemed more desirable the longer we stayed on that beach. Eventually we became almost embarrassed by our European cousins and our own white flesh.

Chris and I still laugh at the incomparable scene on one of the last days of our vacation. We sat on the beach and watched a wealthy and extremely fat German tourist. He was clad only in a G-string and was still untanned. He marched down the beach proudly, brandishing a Maasai spear he had just bought from a beach peddler. These days, the very modest Africans sit and watch almost nude tourists, shake their heads, and privately chuckle at what they see.

The only Africans who bathed in the ocean were athletic young boatmen and fishermen. Pale-skinned Swahili children squatted under shade trees to sell fruit, but I never saw them swim.

Some of the huge luxurious beach houses were owned by Indian businessmen. These families came down in the evening. The men and the children wore swimsuits, but the women wore saris, carried their shoes, and only waded a bit. When the warm water tempted them too much, they sometimes waded in up to the waist for a short time, dragging their nine yards of wet cloth through the water.

After marriage, most modern young Indian girls, used to dressing in skirts, donned saris and affected a new modesty, keeping themselves for their husbands. They usually traveled in family groups, laughing and chattering among themselves but rarely exchanging greetings with strangers.

The Indian women were not the most modest women in Mombasa, however. The Swahili people are descendants of Arab traders who settled the big sea ports along their ancient trade routes. These Arabs brought Islam to these shores and eventually intermarried with coastal people. Along the coast it is quite common to see Moslem women wearing the traditional black covering from head to foot, with only an opening for the kohl-accented black eyes.

Surprisingly, this garb is quite sexual, implying that the owner of these marvelous eyes needs to cover her allures so that she can safely leave her house. Women here are kept secluded in their homes and are very shy. It is almost impossible to sneak a picture of such women, even though they walk the streets of Mombasa to shop or to go to the mosque.

In Mombasa, embarrassed among the Germans, remembering the English colonialists in the highlands, and observing the sari-draped Indian women and black-swathed Swahilis, I realized one thing anew: Kenya's peoples are not all its own. For centuries Kenya has been both target and host for many peoples who have come to settle here for private profit. Over one hundred thousand expatriates live in Nairobi alone. Indians own perhaps a majority of all Kenyan businesses. Many of them have lived in Africa for several generations and call it home. They, and all who import their own strong cultural flavor, affect this tiny nation which is the size of New York State.

When Tanzania declared independence, the Nyerere government nationalized Indian businesses and factories and expelled Indians and other foreigners. They wanted to rid the country of outside influence and learn to be truly Tanzanian—to develop their own solutions. I believe some of the Tanzanian national pride is a result of that determination, although it may have caused economic disaster.

Kenya, on the other hand, is a melting pot. It borders countries with long histories of war, famine, and unrest. These include Ethiopia, Uganda, and Somalia. Tanzania is stable but poor.

Refugees from these countries have flooded Kenya because of its relative stability, available jobs, schools, and hospitals. Political refugees from all over Africa often stop in Kenya, waiting for permanent solutions to their homelessness. European scientists and charitable organizations flock to East Africa because, as one United Nations official put it, "it's a damned zoo."

One warm night our family and our guests gathered driftwood on the deserted beach and lit a big fire. Silently we gazed at the Southern Cross and other unfamiliar constellations. We watched the tiny crabs skitter on the sand. The night outside the circle of flame was inky black and warm. It was a moment heavy in meaning for me.

African life at that moment felt so rich and diverse. The various unique ecologies—coast, highland, alpine, desert, farm, and grassland—all produced different, highly adapted cultures. The exquisite flora and fauna of each brought biologists from all over the world to observe in delight.

The people were as unique and as colorful as the flowers. *That is what I came here to experience*, I thought. *Each of us is a blend of our own uniqueness and the environment, the nurture, surrounding us. God too delights in this blend which produces strength and vigor.* The women of Kenya and Tanzania had many qualities in common. But no two were alike; it was obvious I, too, could learn to celebrate my own place in such a diverse world.

I decided then that I would try to include as many different women and situations as I could in this collection of stories. I had met women in Kenya and Tanzania who represented both village life, with its strong tradition, and the city, with its sophistication. Now I needed to go back and seek out women of the fringe groups, those who did not belong in the mainstream of East African life but *had* colored it.

The veiled women of Mombasa were off-limits. The Maasai women had all been away at a circumcision when I made an expedition to interview them. A tiny, black, Catholic nun who ran a school refused an interview. She was afraid it would make her proud, I think. I was fascinated to learn how the theology of celibacy could be adopted by a culture that worshiped babies.

But there were many others. I decided to look for women who had landed in Kenya almost by accident, women refugees, women minorities. Nairobi, for example, has many such populations.

Perhaps Nairobi is a bit like the coral pool after the ocean has splashed over it, trapping an abundance of life forms, all of them interrelated, no two alike.

2. Yodit—God Was with Me in Prison

Yodit (pronounced Yo'dee; name changed to protect her identity). Born 1963, belongs to a country in turmoil.

Three schoolgirls sat in the interrogation room for the first time, trembling. The government agent had evidently decided to win them over with persuasion instead of force.

"We know you are leaders in that church," he said, frowning. "We know you attend prayer group. And you," he pointed to Yodit, "are attracting young people with that choir of yours. I want it stopped. Don't go there anymore, or I'll have you back here!"

In her typical exuberance, Yodit couldn't resist speaking up. "I know Jesus is true. As long as the church is open and legal, I'll go to it. If the government closes the churches, as people are saying they might, only that will stop me."

The official shook his head in disgust and decided to give the girls a week in jail to teach them a lesson.

After their release, Yodit resumed her twelfth grade studies as best as she could in the charged emotional atmosphere surrounding her and her fellow Christians in 1980. Yodit, her sister Maria, and Maria's friend Meklis, all resumed their work in the church. Yodit taught Sunday school. She also led a youth Bible study and a choir, which attracted non-Christian youth with its fun and lively music.

Government supporters appeared regularly for services to keep tabs on these Christians. They continued to give the girls advice: "This is not good for you. Don't come here!"

Yodit had come from a Coptic background. Coptics stressed Mary and the saints as communicators between God and people. They observed Old Testament Law and pointed to salvation through works. Since moving to the capital city, Yodit had enjoyed a new emphasis on the Bible, Jesus Christ, and grace. She loved the close group of Protestant believers who sang choruses at the top of their lungs. She was born again. She refused to turn back now when God was so close to her.

Five months after the first arrest, Yodit, Maria, and Meklis were arrested again. Again for three days they got political lectures.

"Don't you know politics is the only thing that can change the world? We Communists are the wave of the future. Now raise your left hand and say, 'Destroy Imperialism!' "

The girls looked at each other and shook their heads. They refused. Eighteen-year-old Yodit said, "Sir, as Christians we condemn sin, not people. We will obey the rules of the new government as long as it doesn't touch our Christian principles. But we must obey God first."

Many times the girls were summoned back to prison for a day or two. They all knew that the time was drawing near when they must suffer for Christ's sake. Yodit kept some clothes packed and tried to prepare her widowed mother and six siblings for the inevitable.

One day the three girls felt God telling them that the time was near. They went to church to pray. As they finished praying, a government agent, who had come in quietly as they prayed, said, "Follow me." He took them to a more severe prison than before. About thirty-five men and women from their church fellowship were brought in.

Yodit was taken to a room alone. There the officer sneered. "I am told that at a recent church meeting you raised your hand and requested a song that says, 'God is great; there is no one greater than God! No one can step on me when I have God!' " (This was a popular chorus).

Now Yodit knew that one man of her group must have betrayed her. No one else would have known it was she who had suggested the song. She felt sorrow and pain. One of them had been a spy.

Yodit was forced to do an exercise. Up, down, up, down—until her legs were exhausted. The officer beat her. "No one will step on you? Hah! I will step on you. I will beat you to death."

Time went slowly. Her body was weak, almost numb. She could hardly feel anything. How could she keep getting up and down? The blows continued. Yodit prayed and prayed. She did not cry or scream. She prayed. For an hour and a half Yodit was beaten until her whole body was bloody.

Since she wasn't screaming, the guard yelled, "Can't you feel anything?"

"Yes," she whispered, "my flesh is just like yours. I feel pain. The difference is that I have the love of Christ. He gives me inner strength."

When she staggered out, her group of fellow Christians were crying. Because she had not screamed, they had feared she was already dead. Then her own tears began to flow. Maria had gotten away more easily with a half-hour beating. In their cell, the women collected their clothes to make a mattress for Yodit. They massaged her sore body.

For two months the most stubborn of the Christians were held in prison. Yodit received two more beatings and heard prolonged political discussion.

After one such discussion, the three girls aroused their teacher's anger by proving him wrong. For punishment, the girls had to crawl on their knees over gravel. It was very painful. Yodit kept her mind centered on Jesus and his crucifixion and finally was able to praise God in her heart.

The women slept on the floor of their room. At dawn they would gently touch each other to wake up and to signal a time for silent prayer. Two communist cellmates, imprisoned for "discipline," must not catch on to their forbidden activity. One night they agreed to stay awake all night in silent prayer. In the morning one communist cell-partner shuddered. "I live in the fire these days. It is burning me!"

"Me, all night I couldn't sleep! I have no peace in my heart, and I don't know why," the other replied.

"Maybe these believers were praying last night," the first suggested.

After these two were transferred, the believers were able to pray aloud. They prayed first for a Bible. As they closed their prayer, a prison worker came in and said, "One of the prisoners like you gave me this Bible when he left. Perhaps you'd like to use it?"

From then on, night and day, the fifteen women, all young and unmarried, studied the Bible together. First they read and discussed Acts and later Peter. Yodit will never forget the intensity of that Bible study. The group grew stronger daily. They grew close to each other and to God. All determined to be Bible teachers and house-to-house workers when released.

When Yodit was freed, she had to face the reality of life. Eleventh grade had gone well for her. But this last year, with its jail time and frequent arrests, had ruined her studies. Now she had only one month to study for the matriculation test which would determine if she would go to university. She prayed earnestly that God would help her pass.

In answer to her prayer, God gave Yodit a message in Luke 5:6. Peter had fished all night without good results. But Jesus, in a moment, was able to provide more than enough fish. Jesus was promising Yodit, "Trust me. I will provide more than enough for you."

She failed her test. The next year, after studying on her own, she failed again. The doors to education in her country had closed. Instead, spiritual doors opened. When Yodit prayed for the sick, they improved. When she preached, people listened. She spent hours visiting in homes.

Time and again church leaders offered to pay her as a full-time church worker. "No," she said. "I want to work for the love of God, not for money." She still depends on the gifts of others, and these she sees as gifts from God.

On the streets of her city, Yodit occasionally met the Communist who had betrayed her to the government. When he in turn was imprisoned for discipline, the girls visited him in prison and took a small gift.

Later, meeting on the street, he told Yodit how touched he had been by their forgiveness.

"I am human," she replied. "It's only by God's love we could forgive and love you. You need Jesus, too."

The man listened quietly and asked where he could go to find Christ. Yodit dared not give him her own address. But she did direct him to a church that was still legally open.

She left her country the same week and never saw him again. She hopes that his quest was sincere and he has found peace.

Eventually the government closed Yodit's church. When she felt her work was finished, she accepted a scholarship to a theological college in Kenya that pays her tuition, food, and board. Here she is learning, receiving the education she had prayed for earlier.

"God has a plan for my life," Yodit said. "I'd like to have a good marriage, and sometimes I feel impatient for that. But my first goal is to serve God first all my life. I want to work in the church, live for God. I have no heart to work in the world, to get a job outside the church.

"So I wait. I wait. God has promised to give me 'more than enough.' I know it will all come in his own good time."

Yodit is an attractive, energetic young woman who is surrounded by friends and activity. She is a city girl, dressed in Western-style clothing and heels, her hair curled. She is fervent, prophetic, and intense. She loves to sing and direct choirs. She also has a burden to pray.

Secondarily, she loves children, and they are drawn to her as to a magnet. She teaches Sunday school in a refugee church and loves it. These are the gifts she brings with her in Kenya and wherever else God directs her in the future.

Yodit now has a younger sister with her and a brother in the United States. Maria and another brother are in Germany. They are on their own, unlike the close-knit family life in their home country. Their mother alternately worries and trusts God to protect her far-flung family.

As for Yodit, she is at peace. At age twenty-three, she studies and waits, knowing that in all things God promises her, like Peter, more than enough.

3. Marian—My Children Will Be Muslims

Marian Mohamed Issa. Born 1957, Somali tribe, Gilgil, Kenya. Uganda, Somalia.

Eastleigh, a densely crowded, housing suburb of Nairobi, is home for many Somalis. Many have no legitimate papers and have crowded into Kenya to live among relatives. Others have lived there for years. But they stubbornly retain their separate culture, language, clothes, and religion.

Women with flowing, gauzy, and very feminine robes, their transparent shawls demurely covering their heads, stayed close to home. They sat in the sunshine and knitted, watching as their children played and dodged the little goats that nibbled at piles of garbage. Somali men—lean, handsome, and light-skinned—walked the crowded streets both day and night. They made business deals, chewed *mira,* (a mild stimulant), and held hands with jovial men friends.

Most Somalis are devout and conservative Muslims. There was usually a crowd of men milling outside the corner mosque on Eighth Avenue. I cringed as I passed the loudspeaker—it belched loud Arabic prayers into the already dense soup of blaring horns, bleating goats, and the crowded-street noises of laughter and indignant arguments.

Inside the Eastleigh Community Centre, I met Marian, a pretty twenty-nine-year-old Somali woman in high heels and fashionable clothes. She is a firm Muslim who, ironically, directed a Christian correspondence course which teaches Old Testament Bible to some two thousand students of Muslim background.

"I enjoy working in this environment—the people here are wonderful. My family criticizes my job; they are afraid people here will try to convert me. But what I believe is in my heart. No one can convert someone unless he wants to believe. And no one has ever put pressure on me here.

"There's not much difference between Islam and Christianity. Sometimes I think human error made the differences, not God. If I try to please my God, do what he asks, I don't see why I should worry about being Christian or Muslim. Of course, if my relatives heard me say that, they'd say I was already brainwashed."

Marian felt that the correspondence course taught students to study the Scriptures and examine what they believe.

"We Muslims don't really know the Koran. We go to Koran school, but it is taught in Arabic. We say our prayers in Arabic. When we read the Arabic Koran, it has little meaning to us because it is a foreign language. We have no forum for discussion.

"We say that the Muslims are the most oppressed women in the world. It is because of the way men have interpreted the Koran. The Koran itself is gentle with women."

Marian, if she ever marries, plans to raise her children as good moral Muslims. She spoke of her faith with respect. Yet her involvement in the professional world encouraged obvious lapses of practice, she admitted. She did not cover her head and body as her mother did and as the Koran prescribes. And she had cut her glossy hair into a fashionable perm and wore makeup.

However, she cited the five tenets of Islam: Pray five times a day. Observe the fast of Ramadan. Pay a tithe. Believe in God. Believe in his prophet Mohammed.

"From the time we begin to menstruate until we die, we must pray," she explained. She described the cleansing ceremonies before prayer, the genuflections, and the prayers at 5:30 a.m. and at 1:00, 4:00, 7:00, and 8:00 p.m. Invalids, she said, can genuflect symbolically with their finger if they cannot kneel. But they must still pray.

As she spoke, I heard the *muzzein* calling the faithful to prayer at the corner mosque—a reminder of the claims of God. "On Fridays, our holiday, men and women both go to the mosque, each to his or her own section, to pray. Other days, it is usually the men who go."

Marian, young, intelligent, and obviously an independent thinker, told of her own poor family and fragmented childhood.

"My grandfather left my grandmother because they produced eleven girls. He was frustrated! With his next wife, they produced nine more girls!

"My grandmother was alone and desperate to get her daughters married before they were 'spoiled.' Our people worry a lot about that—the family honor is at stake. Grandmother kept her daughters locked in the house. Not even servants could go in. They had no school, they knew nothing, not even the town they lived in.

"My mother married and had three children. Then she was widowed. She married my father (it was his second marriage, too) and had four more children. When he deserted her, she was already ill with crippling arthritis. The children were sent to live with various relatives.

"I left Gilgil and lived with relatives in Eldoret, Kenya, then in Uganda and Somalia. Finally I returned to Nairobi for high school. Relatives paid my school fees.

"I was the lucky one," she sighed. "My elder sister was tall and beautiful. She was never allowed to go to school. She knew nothing. At fourteen she married a drunkard. Every time she ran away from him, relatives took her back. In this way she bore eight children before she left for good. Now she lives with me, and I help support my crippled mother plus her and her younger children. What kind of a job could she get?"

Marian described health problems this sister suffered, and I suggested a hysterectomy. "Oh, she would never allow that," Marian said vehemently. "She has no knowledge of these things. She would think that was wrong to do to herself. When people do not get out and talk to others or move around in the world, they don't know about many things."

Somali family life is notoriously unstable. A man is allowed four wives at a time, more if he bothers to divorce. Women, too, can remarry up to ten times if they like, as long as they divorce each time.

Formerly, young people were married without knowing each other. Although that is changing rapidly, marriages still tend to occur between congenial families more than as a result of individual choice.

If a wife returns to her family in anger at her husband, the man will eventually seek a go-between, apologize, and pay a *haal*, or fine.

The go-between keeps the money and persuades the woman to return. "Everyone is looking at you and your bad behavior," he might scold her.

"The original grievance is not ventilated or solved," said Marian, "and quarrels usually erupt again. There is no understanding between the partners. Other people interfere. Soon, even though the two may love each other, the marriage dissolves.

"I wouldn't want to be married like my people were," Marian

said sadly, "where there is no understanding in the house. I want to exchange ideas with a husband, to have understanding. But it is hard to find a man like that, especially from my Somali tribe."

In her parents' youth, many Somalis were nomadic. The nomads had more freedom than town women, she said. At night the men and women used to come together to sing, dance and play. They laughed and joked freely with each other. Elopements occurred routinely.

But during the days, men and women stayed strictly separate. Men milked the camels. Then they left early in the morning to go to town, shop, socialize, and sell camels.

Women rose early, took goats out to pasture and milked them, searched for water and carried it long distances in the desert. They cared for children, kept food and fire prepared, moved camp, erected shelters, and watered the camels. "No wonder women felt so oppressed," Marian remembered. "They did all that work."

In a Muslim marriage, the husband vowed to provide food and clothing for his family. The wife was expected to return obedience, bear children, and do the physical work. She stayed well-covered and secluded.

Marian was only one generation removed from this life. She, however, expected to earn money herself, even after marriage. Her world view was entirely different. It was she who supported her family.

"I have two full brothers in the United States. One is a student at Harvard; the other has opened a small shop. They invite me to come and get more education [She has a high school diploma and some college courses.] I may do it someday. I'd like business administration. Formerly, I was an announcer on the Voice of Kenya radio."

How did Marian relate to her many female relatives, I wondered, since most of them did not accept her broadened world view?

"Our families are very close, and we must try to please each other. We visit all the time and offer each other advice. Somalis always cluster together," she said, motioning through the window to the crowded street. "So I try very hard to relate to my family and relatives. I will tell you a story which shows how difficult it can be.

"When I was about eleven I was living with relatives. They arranged for my circumcision. They did not prepare me for this or explain it. There were no ceremonies. They brought in an old woman, almost blind, who used a knife to cut me."

Somalis do not follow the Koran, which prescribes *sunna* circumcision—cutting a slice off the clitoris. Instead, they excise the entire clitoris, cut off the minor labia, and bring the major labia tightly together. They sew the woman shut except for a pencil-sized opening for urine and menstruation. On the wedding night, a midwife will use a knife to cut the woman open. After this she has intercourse with her husband.

There is no anesthesia. The operation is excruciating, especially later when the patient tries to urinate. In Marian's case, the old woman mangled the job and sliced an artery. Marian bled from ten o'clock one morning until two o'clock the next morning. She was almost dead by the time the family called a doctor.

"It was a very bad experience," Marian remembered. "There was no anesthetic. They fed me black tea and bread for days, trying to avoid elimination so I could heal."

She believes that if she has daughters, she will give them sunna circumcision, "like the Koran says."

"You see, in our culture, virginity is terribly, terribly important," she explained. "Mothers are so afraid something bad will happen to their daughters. Then perhaps they could not marry at all. And if they were not circumcised, no man would want them. Their lives would be ruined.

"Mothers do not talk about sex with their daughters. They explain nothing. Girls have to learn when it happens. Also, they never discuss circumcision, even among themselves. Not even now, when so many young women are complaining about their seclusion, their coverings, their circumcision. Some of these more vocal girls have even been cursed by the older women for misleading others."

"Do girls enjoy their weddings?" I asked, knowing that a Somali wedding is an occasion for a big party. "No, I don't think so," Marian said soberly. "They are too scared of what will happen next. Sometimes they didn't choose the man and don't know him well. But everyone wants a child, and a wedding is the way to get one."

Marian had once planned to marry, but family problems intervened and the plans fell through. Now she works, supports her family, and looks around with intelligent curiosity. There is a man she sees regularly.

She said, "My people think that Somalis are the special people. They don't like mixing with others. But I say, everyone has a culture. We all have minds to think. Everyone is special. We are all equal.

"I like to know everything. I like to know how people live!"

4. Kamla—Hindus Pray for Peace Too

Kamla, (not her real name). Born 1946, Jainist Hindu, Indian, Nairobi, Kenya.

A small-boned, attractive woman, Kamla had café-au-lait skin and waist-long, black hair caught in a ponytail. She wore a no-nonsense, cotton sari to her work in a sewing supply and craft shop. This Indian woman and her husband ran the shop, located in modern Nairobi shopping center, together. She consulted him hesitantly before agreeing speak to me.

Over tea she relaxed. We chatted about our roles as wives and mothers. She seemed a bit paranoid, even refusing to let me use her real name. This may simply reflect the closed nature of her Indian community. It is not particularly popular among its African hosts. Indians tread on their adopted soil gingerly, trying not to cause problems.

The immigrant Indian culture, a strong minority in many African nations, reminded me of the European Jewish community before World War II. Like them, the Indians in Africa were urban. They tended to be good business people. They helped each other start new business ventures and corporations and owned many stores, large and small.

Their family structure was important to them and provided a

kind of strength which also closed out outsiders. As with the Jews, religion was a part of their ethnic identity. They did not proselytize, so many people did not have a fair understanding of their morality and belief systems. Perhaps this was because they seemed reluctant or unable to verbalize their beliefs clearly.

Indians usually belonged to one of a variety of Hindu sects, although there were Indian Christian fellowships as well. Among the Hindus, vestiges of the old caste system were still apparent in the arrogance with which shopkeepers ordered their African help and the pittance wages they paid them. Some sects, preoccupied with ritual cleanliness, were careful not to touch the hands of shoppers as money was exchanged.

Thus the Indians, like the Jews, received a significant amount of persecution and misdirected animosity. Some African nations had ousted them and nationalized their businesses, only to regret this when those same industries crumbled.

There were uneasy rumblings in Kenya about their presence and their wealth. We had heard rumors that most Indians were trying to smuggle some of their money out of the country so that if evicted they could start over somewhere else. (A citizen who leaves Kenya may legally take out only several hundred dollars. Kenya doesn't want its currency to leave the country.) The political tension was very real.

As Kamla began to open up and talk about herself, her shyness dropped away. Her warm brown eyes softened. "I am one of about seven thousand Jainist Hindus living here in Nairobi. We are one sect of the Hindu faith—we have our own temple, our own booklets and magazines, our own community which differs from the other Hindus who live here."

She could not tell me how the Jainists differed from other Hindus. She said that there was little teaching in the temple. It was a place to gather, to sing, and to pray. The teaching mostly took place at home.

"Our community is very close. There were 2500 guests for both lunch and dinner at my sister's wedding. The celebration lasted several days. When we have small family parties on holidays, we usually have forty or fifty guests, including aunts, uncles and cousins.

"Our families have traditionally been large. My mother-in-law, for example, would not accept any form of family planning. She thought that was blocking souls from being born and was a sin against God. I myself was one of six children. But I have only two daughters, age fourteen and seventeen. So you see, times are changing. Children are too expensive to raise these days, and I was in favor of birth control.

"Then too, the majority of Indian women stay at home. I'm an exception. We are changing, but I believe our culture changes more slowly than yours. Our men like to make the decisions. They have the responsibility to look after the family. The women stay at home, have children, and care for the home, often with the aid of helpers.

"My mother always accepted everything my father suggested. He always had a lot of life, vitality. I didn't see that in my mother. She just accepted everything. The older women tolerated a lot and did most of the work. Me, I'm not like that, although I admit I admire my parents' togetherness.

"In our family we always valued education. There were about twenty-five in my family, including grandparents, uncles, and cousins. As we grew up, we got training. My parents valued our education, even for girls, more than housework. But after our education was finished, they still expected a girl to come back into the home as a housewife."

As Kamla spoke, I pictured the many Indian women I saw as they shopped and chattered in small groups, surrounded by their children. Most kept carefully out of the sun and stayed in the house. This gave them a peaked and unmuscled look. Their husbands shared the look, caused by hunching over shop counters for long hours each day.

The women tended to get overweight quickly but still groomed themselves carefully. They brushed their uncut, thick hair carefully and wore saris with glittery edgings and brilliant designs. The short blouses they wore as tight as they could. Their bare midriffs showed tantalizingly beneath the sari drapery.

The Indian community ranged from middle to upper class in the African countries. Its members often lived in lush, flowered suburbs in white-washed houses. There were separate servants quarters.

Others, however, occupied modest apartment houses which were almost squalid by American standards. They attended temples whose domes sparkled white in the city skylines, with gold-gilded carvings and mosaics of intricate Oriental design.

Popular Indian rock music usually whined from matatu radios. It was particularly annoying to Western ears not used to Oriental half-tones and twanged notes.

Gourmets learned to enjoy the Indian cuisine served in many restaurants, although it was extremely hot and spicy. A great variety of vegetarian dishes, chutneys, and sauces were always served at one meal. This must have kept those housebound women cooking for most of their lives.

Grocery shelves were heavily stocked with dozens of curry powders and special spices. Chris and Lisen loved *samosas*, a curried meat wrapped in bread dough and deep fried, a typical lunch snack available everywhere.

Kamla was a different style altogether from the typical Indian wife; she was agile and compact and dressed in a simple sari. Obviously she was a do-er, a businesswoman who thrived on challenges.

"After I finished school I became a nurse at Aga Khan Hospital. My parents respected nursing, although many Indian families look down on it as a dirty job. I enjoyed the work, but after one comes to a certain age, one no longer enjoys having other people telling you what to do. So I began looking around.

"Both grandfathers had businesses, so it was natural for me to think about opening a shop. That is what I did. I'm more independent now. And of course, one earns more money by working for oneself. My husband and I enjoy working together to run this business.

"My great-grandparents came to Kenya from North India when my grandfather was a young boy. They began a business here. So I'm a fourth-generation Kenyan. If I were to go to India, I'd be lost.

"Up to now, we were confident we were Kenyan citizens. My children thought they were automatic citizens. But now the students are having trouble with their passports when they apply to go abroad to university. We are no longer sure if they will be allowed to remain here in the future.

"There are big questions. I have been to England three times, and many of my family are there. So we are perhaps international, not belonging to any one country.

"My elder daughter wants to go to school in England. I think that will be good for her. She has been with me for seventeen years. I've always talked to her about life; we are like friends. I trust her. I have people there, of course, who will take her in.

"I trust that my daughter is well grounded in our family's values. We Indians don't get absorbed into the culture around us. We have always kept our own language, dress style, and religion. I don't think my daughters will change either.

"Our way of looking at the world is important to us. We believe that nothing happens because you *made* it happen. Rather, whatever happens was destined to happen.

"If I live a good or a bad life, a *karma* develops around me. This will influence not only me but my descendants. My life now is influencing the future. And whatever was done in past generations is partly molding my life now. So if I am successful, it is partly because of my family's luck, or karma.

"We are nonviolent people. In the house we walk barefoot so we don't kill as many ants underfoot. We don't kill any creature, so we are usually vegetarians. We believe that life is eternal—it will go on whether we die or not. Our lives do not end when we die.

"This is a hard thing to teach our children, but we talk straight to them. We play them tapes, tell them stories, we teach them. Our religion makes us close to each other. We teach, 'Don't cheat people.' That is important. We teach people to be frank, honest, open in their dealings."

"Doesn't this fatalistic attitude—that people suffer because of their own or their family's past sins—encourage Hindus to accept injustice and pain rather than change it?" I was puzzled. "It must be easy to think, 'Well they must be paying for their sins,' when you see suffering."

Kamla shrugged. "Perhaps, to a degree. But we too try to contribute to the community, to improve things. We contribute to the Aga Khan Hospital. We sponsor things like Peace Day, to encourage people to pray for world peace.

"But I admit there is a big gap between Indians and Kenyans. We are not close, and our ideas about life are different. We mostly don't understand or even like each other. So we keep to ourselves except when we work together.

"We women are mostly satisfied to be close to our family members, children, our husband's parents, and the members of the Indian community."

CHAPTER

The Story-tellers

1. Our Family on the Road

Just today I listened again to tapes our family made in cars and motel rooms scattered across Kenya and Tanzania. As Bob and the children reported back home, their conversations were full of adventures and names of new friends, new places, new things learned. But there were also comments betraying that their experiences were stressful.

Lisen: "We are in a nice hotel. It has room service. That is really neat because we can eat in our room, and nobody will stare at us!"

Another time, in a voice of jubilation, "Guess what our hotel room has? A REAL TV! Of course, it doesn't work. When you turn it on it just goes 'Bzzzt.' "

"I miss Nana. I miss King, our dog. I want to go home."

Chris: "Mom dragged us out to the village every day this week to work. She goes into the houses to meet people and I sit in the car in the heat. The seats are vinyl and after awhile I am all sweaty. And all these kids come and just gather to stare at me. Twenty-five is the record number of little kids so far. It's uncomfortable, to say the least."

"We had nine people in our little Fiat today. It was hot. Mom comes back tired and her personality is 'nasty!' "

"We are staying in a nice guest house, only there is a sink in my bedroom and two scorpions crawled out."

Bob: "I'm worried about my health. I've been sick while we are traveling, with a fever and chills and stomach pains. Finally we got to a Western doctor who thinks I have an amoeba of the upper gastrointestinal tract. After three days of medication I feel hungry again, and I think I stopped losing weight. I've lost thirty pounds since I arrived in Africa."

"Well, we are on our way home to Nairobi from a successful month in Tanzania. We are in a motel with real hot water. You don't know what that means until you've washed with cold water for a whole month. Lisen spent an hour in the bathtub. It's the first time I felt clean in a month!

"The month in Tanzania was wonderful in many ways, but it was hard on me because I was worried about germs. The mission pumped lake water to the houses. Then every morning we filled our water filter and boiled filtered lake water for drinking. It tasted fishy to me, and I could hardly drink it. I know how polluted the lake is, with bilharzia and everything. I washed our clothes by hand in cold water, so I never felt our clothes were very clean either."

Anyone who has ever vacationed with a family knows that being cooped up together in cars and motel rooms and eating strange food is not all it's cracked up to be. We all did our best, but sometimes it all got to be too much.

One of those times happened on one of our early trips to Kisumu in western Kenya. The hotels we could afford were shoddy. People stared at us when we ate. The climate by the lake was hot and humid. Our car was always overcrowded, the trunk filled with all our worldly possessions and the inside with bodies.

One afternoon, after we had dropped everyone off, Bob said he couldn't wait to get back to our hotel room and shut the door. He would eat in the room. I, too, was hungry and hot. But I did not relish the hotel food.

"Can't we stop and eat some curry in that small restaurant?" I asked.

Bob and the kids groaned. "Okay, you go inside and see if they really have any curry," Bob said.

"What do you mean? It's advertised on the sign!" I said, indignantly. I went inside alone. Not bad. The little restaurant was almost empty. The big sign advertised three kinds of curry. A few locals were eating there.

I went back outside and ushered the family in. "Looks good," I said. All four of us trooped in and sat down. Everyone stared at us, of course, but no one came. Finally I went to a front counter and asked for chicken curry and rice.

"We don't have any left," the waiter said, shrugging. I went down the menu. It seemed everything had been sold out. They were ready to close. No one apologized. They were too interested in watching us.

We left. When we got back inside the car I could feel the steam rising from Bob's head. I tried to make a joke about the whole thing. No one laughed.

By now, sunset had cast pink, yellow, and blue-gray shadows into the clouds and these were reflected on Lake Victoria.

Chris got his camera out. "Dad, can you get back to our hotel room quick so that I can take a picture?" (On the fourth floor we had a great view of the lake, over rusty tin rooftops.)

Chris and Lisen wrangled in the back seat, hot and irritated. Bob dodged potholes, and Chris urged him to hurry. I mourned the curry I was starved for and grumped in the front seat about the aggravating restaurant. By the time we got back to the hotel and clumped up the many stairs to our room, the sunset was gone.

"Take the picture anyway," Bob roared to a frustrated Chris. "I don't care if it's dark. Take the stupid picture!"

After room service brought us mediocre food with wonderful pots of hot, sweet tea and heated milk and we took showers in cold water, we revived enough to start laughing. We immortalized the catastrophe by making a hilarious tape to take home in which we verbalized all our frustrations and exaggeratedly blamed each other for our terrible day.

My body was charged with adrenaline and happiness. I did not have a single day of sickness except for the mild diarrhea that seemed to be a fact of life there. The first time I got sick was the day we were to return to the States; I spent the day throwing up.

Bob, on the other hand, had several crises to deal with, usually when I was absent. He developed an abscessed tooth and was deathly ill after its extraction. Driving home on dangerous, unlit roads late that night, he almost fainted.

Another time I stayed at the coast while he and the children boarded the night train to Nairobi to meet visiting relatives from the States. The family had eaten shrimp from our own refrigerator (which did not work well) for supper. That night Lisen was the first to develop food poisoning, followed by Chris and then Bob. Alone, he had to deal with violently sick children throwing up into the tiny train sink.

The most serious and long-lasting sickness was his amoebic dysentery, which left him thin and weak, without much endurance. We all took preventive medicine for malaria and slept under mosquito nets when outside Nairobi. We were grateful that none of us contracted it.

All of this is included to admit and acknowledge our humanness as a family. There were hard times and growing experiences. Bob and I had exchanged roles, and both of us struggled to make our relationship work.

Yet as I listen to the tapes and reread letters and diary journals I find so much richness in that year for each member of the family.

Bob: "I spent the whole afternoon talking with a pastor today. Together we went to visit a second pastor. We discussed the leadership problems in the Kenyan church and the dissension that is tearing the church apart right now. The elder pastor was in tears as he admitted his own anger and disappointments. We prayed together; it was a very moving time. I was glad to feel that they really accepted me and appreciated my willingness to listen."

"I spoke today with a pastor who said, 'I'm afraid it is very hard for Westerners to understand the Holy Spirit.' "

Chris: "I've had my soccer ball all year long. It means a lot to me because often, when I was alone, it was the only thing to do. I really wanted to keep that ball, to remember what this year was like. But today I gave it away. It was hard, but I'm glad I did. The boy I gave it to had no toys."

Lisen, in her diary: "I love Africa. I love the flowers. And we get to stay a whole year!"

"I met a friend today. Her name is Sallie. She is black."

"I learned to swim today. I can lie down in the water, and I don't drown!"

None of us will ever forget the experience of the game parks, Mount Kenya, Mombasa, and the Indian Ocean. But foremost, the year was one in which we stretched to know and enjoy people different from ourselves.

Yes, that involved stress sometimes. But both Chris and Lisen met a big world in which so many American preoccupations simply had no place. In this world were no house-furnishing magazines, no clothing catalogs, no big department-store sales, no Christmas decorations, no junk mail. There were no brand-name status symbols and no public references to sex. It was a year for touching the essenials—our relationships with God and each other.

In short, our experiences were both hard and wonderful. Now, a year later, when a PBS special comes on TV, Lisen will complain, "I'm tired of Africa." But if she hears a Swahili word she knows she is excited. "I heard someone say 'mbili'!" she will say.

Chris occasionally gets homesick for both people and places. He talks of going back. So do I.

Bob, on the other hand, remembering amoebas, shakes his head. "It was an excellent experience," he will say, "but I'm not ready yet to go back."

All four of us are different people. We brought home with us individual gifts from Africa. We are far richer now than we were before.

2. Taping the Stories

On Palm Sunday, 1987, Bob and I spent most of the day running back and forth to the airport. We made frantic phone calls to other countries to track down missing persons. We passed out aspirin to women who had flown for the first time and had arrived utterly exhausted. But by evening, we had assembled a group who would live together for the next two weeks and become a family.

These women represented eight language groups and had already translated twenty of the stories I had collected into their own language. Now, together in Nairobi, we were going to read the stories onto tape and finish the project.

"Tell the stories in your own way," I urged them. "The story is meant for your own people. Tell the story in a way that they would appreciate."

Arnie Newman, an electronics expert and dedicated missionary, was our mainstay. He rigged up a soundproof room, hung with colorful kangas to absorb noise. He brought his professional, portable equipment to an Anglican retreat center we had rented in the Nairobi highlands.

Epampia Mbo Wato, a single man in his twenties, had escorted two women from Zaire. Although French was their main language, he also knew English, as well as four trade languages. We were all undyingly grateful for Epampia, who handled being surrounded by all these women with tact and grace. His humor and cheerfulness saved many a day.

Bob and Chris ran errands, took women sightseeing and shopping all over Nairobi, and ran in and out as needed. The rest of us lived and slept in a large room, combed each other's hair, took turns in the little bathroom, and immersed ourselves in typical, feminine dorm life.

Rebecca Osiro was eight and a half months pregnant. I prayed that the baby would wait until she had taped the Luo stories. She did. Rebecca was the youngest woman, and all of us teased her about her pregnancy, which delighted her.

Loyce Chacha was a bit older, mother of five, and an English and Swahili teacher in Dar es Salaam, Tanzania. She had a cynical smile, a joke for every occasion and was a bit of a rebel. She pretended not to take the world seriously.

Doris Dube had left her eighteen-month-old twins and other children at home. A veteran radio worker and teacher back in Zimbabwe, Doris was a joy to work with. She had been collecting women's stories before she heard of me, and we felt God had helped us find each other.

Rachel Mushala, of Zambia, was older, wise, and in poor health. She had a gentleness that allowed her to get away with giving the younger women good advice.

Kadi Hayalume, from Zaire, had the most education; she had graduated from a seminary. She also had the most flamboyant personality. I could have written a novel about her. She was upset because she had just discovered she was pregnant for the seventh time. She calmed herself with long, beautiful French prayers.

Themua Mbualungu, also from Zaire, was dignified; she was used to being a women's leader and politician. She enjoyed argument and discussion about church doctrine. During the conference, her weak heart scared us. The doctor overmedicated her, giving her a bad reaction. She was the only one who didn't finish taping her stories.

This group of women and Epampia worked hard for two weeks; each got one hour of taping time per day. The rest of the day was spent polishing translations, practicing reading the stories, and relating to each other.

Unfortunately, it was the cold, rainy season. The highlands air was quite damp, the temperature in the sixties. We bribed a caretaker to build us big, roaring fires in the library. The Zairians, especially, were appalled at such cold weather and prayed that God would protect them from pneumonia.

Each night we had devotions and sang together. We prayed in our own languages; it always seemed like Pentecost, since no two of us had the same language. Together we ate the Kenyan menus—food the other Africans did not always like. They craved their own foods.

When electricians showed up to do some renovations at the retreat center, noises of hammering and sawing soon filtered into our taping room. Even worse, the electricity was turned off frequently, driving Arnie crazy. Power surges ruined my typewriter. Hot water for baths was scarce.

But on the very last day all of us but Themua did finish. It was close. We had all begun guarding our taping time, because each woman wanted to finish a complete story set. Even Rachel, when asked to exchange times with another woman, asserted with big eyes, "It's MY TURN!"

On Easter Sunday a local women's group cooked a big meal. We spent a long afternoon sharing about how women's groups operate in the various countries.

We were invited to sing in church. This was a problem, because we all knew different songs, each in her own language. Finally someone hummed, "Up From the Grave He Arose." This proved a universal Easter favorite. We sang the verses in Tonga, Ndebele, Kituba and Swahili. We invited the congregation to join in the chorus. We sang enthusiastically in our own languages. Another Pentecost experience. Christ had again bridged cultural gaps.

We took communion together the last night. Mama Themua, the only elder among us, passed it out formally, her hands shaking. We prayed, then made little speeches.

"I always dreamed that we women would someday be able to reach out and get to know other Christians in other countries. Now I have had that chance. I want the stories to do that for others," one said.

"Thank you, Mary, for bringing us together," another said.

"You have given the African women a real gift by collecting these stories. It wouldn't have happened if you hadn't gotten things started," said another.

All of us had been deeply touched by our weeks together and by our mutual goals for our fellow-women. We knew that only the Holy Spirit's power had overcome the obstacles to creating the tapes. We knew, too, that it was only a beginning. Much more needs to be done with women around the world until poverty, illiteracy, and injustice are conquered. But first we must understand each other. That will bring love. And love is the prerequisite to any lasting solutions.

The Author

Mary Lou Cummings (left) and Mana Tshimuna, a village teacher.

Mary Lou Cummings is a freelance writer and editor who has spent a lifetime listening to people. In 1986 she approached Mennonite Central Committee (MCC), a relief agency, with her dream of enabling African women to listen to each other. She would do this by recording their stories on tape.

One year later, after her extensive travel in five countries and with the help of many local volunteers, interpreters, and storytellers, the set of tapes became available in eight languages through MCC.

Mary Lou is married to Robert Cummings, a science teacher, who participated actively in her African project. With their two children, seventeen-year-old Chris and eleven-year-old Lisen, they live in the home Bob built among the woods and boulders of Quakertown, Pennsylvania.

Mary Lou is active in the Perkasie Mennonite Church. She edits *The Franconia Conference News* and several smaller publications.

She is a former English and creative writing teacher. She received a B.A. from Bluffton College (Bluffton, Ohio) in 1966 and an M.A. from Temple University (Philadelphia, Pa.) in 1968. She was the editor of *Full Circle: Stories of Mennonite Women* (Faith and Life Press, 1978).